O. M
12/93

DATE DUE

~~DE 17 '95~~	~~JE 15 05~~		
~~DE 1 95~~	~~FE 16 05~~		
~~SE 13 '96~~	~~AP 20 05~~		
~~OC 15 '96~~			
~~NO 5 '96~~			
~~RENEW~~			
~~OC 2~~			
~~NO 3 '97~~			
~~NO 25 '98~~			
~~OC~~			
~~AP 30 04~~			
~~MY 24 05~~			

DEMCO 38-296

BLACK DANCE

BLACK DANCE

Edward Thorpe

THE
OVERLOOK
PRESS

To all those Black dancers whose life and work went unrecorded.

First published in 1990 by
The Overlook Press
Lewis Hollow Road
Woodstock, New York 12498

Library of Congress Cataloging-in-Publication Data

Thorpe, Edward.
  Black dance.

  Bibliography: p.
  Includes index.
    1. Blacks – Dancing – History. 2. Afro-Americans –
Dancing –
history. 1. Title.
  GV1603.T49 1990 792.8089'96073   89-8785

ISBN 0 – 87951 – 379 – 9

Contents

Author's Note

'There is no such thing as Black dance!' This characteristically mischievous remark came from Geoffrey Holder, the dancer, choreographer and designer born in Trinidad, when I interviewed him in New York. What he meant, I think, is that there is no specifically notated form of Black dance in the manner of classical ballet or the Martha Graham style of modern dance. And he inferred that Black dance, inasmuch as its roots are in African tribal customs, has been absorbed into white western entertainment idioms, or adapted to formal presentation in the white theatrical tradition, which has robbed it of its identity.

It is pointless to argue the matter. There remains, however, the propensity of Black people to dance, and dance in a manner specifically derived from those African roots – it is in the blood, bones and soul of the Afro-Caribbeans, however westernised they have become.

It is the purpose of this book to chronicle the development of that 'propensity to dance' as a major contribution to both Black and white cultures. It does not set out to be comprehensive – such a definitive record would run to several volumes – nor does it attempt an anthropological analysis of Black tribal history in dance terms. My intention has been to chart the main course of Black dance in a white world, to touch, briefly, on its African origins and point to a number of prominent features in a large, often uncharted, terrain of achievement.

In researching the book I must acknowledge a dichotomy between Black dancers. There are those who are very conscious of their Black cultural history, whose performances and choreography seek to formalise Black dance as something conceptually distinct from white culture. And there are those who resent being labelled Black dancers, who say, 'I am a dancer; the colour of my skin is irrelevant.' I respect and accept both attitudes and, indeed, they are not irreconcilable. As another distinguished Black dancer, choreographer, teacher and archivist, Joe Nash, said to me, 'It's just fine that they have the freedom to make the choice.'

J. G. S. Sauveur inv. direx.   J. Laroque Sculp.

Guiriot ou Jongleur du Senegal

1

Slavery

The emancipation of slaves throughout the British Empire came into force in 1833. Slavery was abolished in the French colonies in 1848, by the Dutch in 1863 and in the USA in 1865, during the Civil War. Even so, Black people in the western world have remained enslaved by the forces of politics, prejudice and poverty.

The traditional means of escape from these social evils have been by way of entertainment and sport and by far the most potent element in these routes to freedom has been dance. Dance – the expressive movement of the head, torso, limbs and feet – is as natural and instinctive to the Afro-Caribbean races as conversation. Practically every human emotion – joy, sorrow, anger, fear, pity, religious ecstasy – is habitually displayed in daily discourse through dance by the tribes of West Africa which provided by far the greatest number of slaves for the Caribbean and the American mainland.

In 1935 Geoffrey Gorer wrote in *Africa Dances*: 'Africans dance. They dance wonderfully. The Singhalese, the Balinese, the Cambodians dance more subtly, more dramatically; but as far as I have seen their range is limited and their invention small compared with the Negroes. Africans have only one art (sic) but to what a pitch they have brought it! First and last Africans dance.'

The ability and propensity of the Africans to dance has, of course, been chronicled at length over some four centuries or more, not least by men associated with the slave trade. As early as the beginning of the sixteenth century African slaves were being transported to Haiti. A hundred years later nearly a million slaves had reached the West Indies and the numbers steadily increased during the next two centuries. It was common practice for the slaves to be taken first to the West Indies and the islands of the Caribbean where, for some years they were 'seasoned', then to be transported to the American mainland, usually to be sold for work in the cotton plantations of the southern states.

During the horrendous sea journey from West Africa, during which

◀ *An eighteenth-century print of a professional dancer in Senegal.*

it was commonplace for nearly fifty per cent of the slaves to die under the cramped, filthy, disease-ridden conditions below decks, the pathetic human cargo was – weather permitting – brought on to the open decks and made to dance. This was partly to afford exercise and so keep the slaves relatively healthy (the dead and dying were thrown overboard) and partly to afford entertainment for the crew; below decks the men were shackled while the women were allowed to roam free at the mercy of the crew. Often the slaves were forced to dance by being lashed with whips; others, on ships which were 'well-run', danced from their own volition, glad of the fresh air and the opportunity to express their feelings. Many of their dances and the songs which sometimes accompanied them were, naturally, lamentations at being taken from their homeland and separated from their families.

On the less 'well-run' ships the slaves were often made to 'dance' (in reality it was jumping up and down) while still chained in their quarters. Those who did not perform satisfactorily were flogged.

Not infrequently it was through dance that many slaves were first enticed on board; rewards were offered to perform their tribal dances as entertainment, then, when the dancing was over, they were taken below, given intoxicating drinks, and when they awoke from an alcoholic stupor found themselves far out to sea.

Most of the on-deck dances were performed to the beat of a drum or some makeshift substitute. Occasionally the sailors themselves would provide the music with a banjo, fiddle, pipes or even a harp; more often it was just a tambourine. The drum, of course, was and still is the chief instrument for African dances; the structural complexities of African rhythms, frequently created by a number of drums in elaborate counterpoint, are highly sophisticated, but in the confines of a ship they were usually simple. In the absence of any instrument the rhythm would be beaten out on anything to hand: cooking utensils, boxes, ship's equipment. The propensity of the African to dance would not be defeated by

▼ *A late eighteenth-century print illustrating how slaves were transported below decks.*

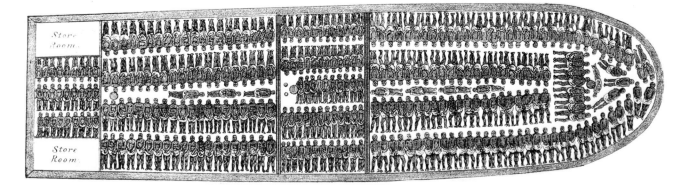

▲ *Weather permitting, slaves were regularly brought on deck to dance in order to keep them healthy. Those who were reluctant to perform were forced to do so under the lash.*

the lack of any instrument; if all else failed hand-clapping would more than suffice.

The dances themselves ranged from set pieces, such as a war dance or courting ceremonial, to Ring Dances and impromptu solos. On some of the Spanish ships which were, generally speaking, the worst run of all the slave ships, the dances frequently descended into exhibitions of 'lewdness', with orgiastic scenes taking place between the sailors and the female slaves.

Once ashore the abilities and opportunities of the slaves to dance were given greater latitude, particularly in the Caribbean. Those islands which fell under French and Spanish influence provided a relatively greater degree of 'freedom' to the slaves to pursue their instincts to dance, not least because of the attitudes of the Catholic church. Its object was the salvation of the Black man's soul, not the persecution of his culture. Only when his so-called 'heathen' religious rites, often expressed in dance, were involved did the church react repressively. By contrast the Protestant denominations were far more repressive, not to say destructive of Black culture: in the Catholic-dominated West Indies the Black man was considered a human being, albeit with very few rights; on mainland America he was usually regarded as subhuman and treated with cruel and callous indifference.

The usual transportation of 'seasoned' slaves from the West Indies to the American mainland was increased in 1803 after the insurrection of the slaves in Haiti under their military leader Toussaint l'Ouvature. With continuing warfare, during which the French and Spanish governments tried to win back their lost possessions, many of the white settlers and their slaves fled to Louisiana, particularly New Orleans, thus establishing the large Black community in that city where, after the abolition of slavery, the Black culture of dance and its syncopated rhythms was able to flourish.

For the slaves of New Orleans there was considerable liberality, leading to the establishment of what might be considered a 'Black aristocracy', particularly after intermarriage; some of the Creoles became plantation owners and had their own slaves (see chapter 16 on Dance Theater of Harlem). But whatever the social standing of the Black families, whether they came direct from the African continent or entered into a liaison with the white settlers, Black dance had taken root in America.

2

Dance Forms

The dances practised by the West African tribes who formed the mass of slaves transported to the Caribbean and mainland America ranged from simple, impromptu solos to elaborate religious rituals. In performance they varied accordingly, from shuffling and stamping to frenzied shaking that involved the whole body, head to toe.

The basic difference between Black dances and those performed by the white races is in the degree of articulation – as can be seen on almost any disco floor. In most dances performed by whites, whether they be folk dances, social dances, court dances or the highly elaborate and 'artificial' techniques of classical ballet, the torso is held comparatively erect, if not rigid, the head and shoulders, limbs and feet giving whatever amount of expression may be intended. Sometimes the virtuosity is emphasised in the feet as in, for example, Scottish reels, Celtic clog dances, Spanish flamenco or Slavic mazurkas. Sometimes the movements are deliberately slow and graceful as in the minuet, or fast, as in the volta; but in every case the torso is 'pulled up'. It may sway or bend a little, the shoulders may lift and turn in counterpoint with the hips but, compared to Black dances, the movement is minimal.

In Black dance the pelvic region is the epicentre of all movement: it may thrust back and forth or rotate in simulation of the reproductive act (though that form of replication is more often in the eye of the beholder than the executant); it may shake and shimmy from side to side and transmit these vibratory, gyratory movements to almost every other joint in the body, the back, the shoulders, neck, elbows, knees and ankles, so that the performer seems almost convulsed or galvanically charged. Whereas the dances of the white races are so often concerned with conveying grace, dignity, pride or elegance, with Black dance the concern is not with the self-conscious presentation of something 'beautiful' for the onlooker to observe, but almost wholly with what is felt, what emotion is being experienced by the dancer himself. *The beauty of Black dance lies in its total lack of inhibition.*

Again and again, throughout the centuries, western observers, from missionaries to sea captains, anthropologists to consular officials, have referred to the tribal dances of West Africa as 'lewd', 'libidinous', 'lascivious', 'disgusting' and 'hideous', imposing their own pre-determined ideas of what constitutes a socially acceptable vocabulary of movement on to an alien culture. That it can have an erotic content is indisputable – but then so can western dance in all its forms: In 1816 an editorial in *The Times* inveighed with passion against the 'indecent foreign dance called "The Waltz"'. Be that as it may, it would seem that from the beginning of slavery until the present day all forms of Black dance have intrigued and excited the white races and in many instances Black instinctual forms of movement have been incorporated into more formalised western dances.

The variety of Black dance forms is tremendous. The Africans of the Gold Coast were more warlike than most of the inland tribes and their dances abound with ferocious confrontations between the men, while the farmers and shepherds of the interior regions, such as the Senegalese and Congolese, enjoyed their dances more as a form of relaxation than as a threat to their neighbours, and their movements are sensual rather than vigorous.

One of the favourite dances which reappeared amongst the slaves of the West Indies was the Calenda, a dance which was particularly frowned upon by slave owners and missionaries because of its 'immodesty'. The men and women faced each other in two lines and danced to an impromptu song made up by one of the bystanders, the refrain taken up by other bystanders and the rhythm provided by hand-clapping. Holding their arms in a crescent, rather like Spanish castanet players, or in the open fifth position of classical ballet, the lines of dancers advanced upon each other, sometimes jumping, sometimes making swift turns until they were within a few feet of each other, then they retreated; advancing once more, the dancers made contact, slapping their thighs together, kissing and making 'lascivious gestures'. As the dance progressed the pace became faster, the contacts more sensual. One observer of the Afro-Caribbean dances in the eighteenth century wrote that 'the Blacks would willingly pass entire days at this exercise', but by the middle of the century the Calenda had been banned by many plantation owners because they feared that its incendiary nature might lead to uprisings amongst the native population. Even so it continued to be danced throughout the West Indies and on the mainland of America. The Spanish Creoles in Louisiana were particularly fond of it and there is even a record of it being performed by nuns to 'record their joy at the birth of the saviour'.

An eighteenth-century print showing a Black couple performing the Chica on the island of Martinique. It is interesting to note that the artist, presumably French, makes no attempt to caricature the dancers.

The Calenda existed under several different names, such as the Kalenda, the Jo-and-Johnny, the Joan-and-Johnny and a version, the Caleinda, performed by males only, stripped to the waist and twirling heavy sticks in a mock fight, which must have been rather different to the 'indecent' versions performed by mixed couples.

Another dance that was very popular and which may have originated with the Congolese was the Chica. Recorded in the Windward Islands and Santo Domingo it reached as far as New Orleans and Cuba. It would seem that the dance began with a single female, holding the ends of her skirt or a handkerchief; to a pronounced rhythm she would sway the lower part of her body while holding the torso relatively still; after a while a man would enter the arena, moving forward towards the woman, lunging provocatively, drawing back, throwing himself forward again precipitously until, to quote one chronicler of the time, 'When the Chica reaches its most expressive stage, there is in the gestures and in the movements of the two dancers a harmony which is more easily imagined than described.'

We may infer that both the Calenda and the Chica were mating dances in which the executants were incited to more and more intimate contact and in which the initial couples were progressively joined by others. Anthropologists suggest that elements of the Chica later surfaced in the Rumba and the Mambo.

One of the instruments which accompanied the Chica was a drum called the Bamboula and there are references to a dance of the same name; descriptions of the dance, however, lead one to assume that it is the same as the Chica, one of the several instances of a particular dance or dance rhythm going under a different title.

One of the most important dances that appeared throughout the whole of the Caribbean islands and the American south was the Juba. Unlike the Calenda and Chica, which were provocatively erotic, the Juba was in essence a competition dance, a dance of technical skill which included 'cadenzas' of personal virtuosity.

It is worth quoting from F. W. Wurdemann's vivid account, published in 1844, of the Juba performed by negro slaves in Cuba:

> Presently a woman advances and commencing a slow dance, made up of shuffling of the feet and various contortions of the body, thus challenges a rival from among the men. One of these, bolder than the rest, after awhile steps out, and the two then strive which shall first tire the other; the woman performing many feats which the man attempts to rival, often excelling them, amid the shouts of the rest. A woman will sometimes drive two or three successive *beaux* from the ring, yielding her place at length to some impatient *belle*, who has been meanwhile looking on with envy at her success. Sometimes a sturdy fellow will keep the field for a long time, and one after another of the other sex will advance to the contest only to be defeated; each one, as she retires, being greeted by the laughter of the spectators.

We may assume that the 'shuffling of the feet' was, in fact, the preparatory establishment of a chosen rhythm, not the inexpert execution of the steps that the phrase implies.

▲ *A John Canoe dancer,
drawn by the author after
an original sketch appearing in a journal in 1929.
Such elaborate head-
dresses inhibited the performance of the dance
somewhat.*

*(over) Black dancers,
accompanied by drum
and tambourine, per-
forming for a white audi-
ence on the island of St
Dominique.*

There are records of the Juba being performed in the Bahamas by men only, openly competitive, each one adding and extending his own steps, leaps and movements which were his particular *forte*, a series of bravura solos which continued throughout the night.

The Calenda, Chica and Juba are but three of many dances which may be termed social dances. Other dances which were equally wide-spread throughout the Caribbean were ceremonial dances, holiday dances and religious dances.

One of the ceremonies that embraces both holiday festivities and religious observance is the appearance of the John Canoe dancers. The origin of the name is obscure but is thought to refer to one John Conny, a *cabocero* or headman from the West African coast, who was celebrated around 1720. The John Canoe dancers appeared during the Christmas festivities (although the custom survives in New Orleans as part of Mardi Gras) and their appearance was heralded for several weeks by the regular beating of the *gombay* drum (sometimes written *gumbé*, *goombay* or *gamby*). The men were dressed in strange clothes, carried wooden swords and on the head of each one was a pair of ox horns emerging from a fearsome mask which also had large tusks. The dancers stopped at every door, shouting 'John Canoe!' at the top of their voices. They were usually accompanied by a retinue of drunken women. The women, for some obscure reason, were divided into the Reds and the Blues, two rival factions each led by a queen wearing clothes of the appropriate colour. In the nineteenth century the head-dresses of the men became much more elaborate and sophisticated, the horns and tusks giving way to pasteboard houses which contained puppets and dolls.

There seems to be very few descriptions of the actual John Canoe dance and it is likely that the complex headdresses precluded any very forceful or violent movement, although the men seem to have 'gyrated' frequently while the women affected a 'gambolling' progress. Money was collected from those who watched the ceremony to pay for the feasting which followed: an example of a Black ceremonial of uncertain origin attaching itself to a Christian memorial.

A similar ritual to the John Canoe dancers were the Gombay dancers of Bermuda who also appeared during the Christmas period. These were formed by males only, masked with the visages of ferocious beasts, as well as carefully constructed models of ships and houses. The movements of the Gombay dancers were executed in a circle; at the climax a few leading dancers would detach themselves from the ring and throw themselves about in a fervent manner, sometimes writhing on the ground in feverish ecstasy, the drumming also reaching a furious climax.

Throughout the West Indies the plantation slaves were allowed to perform their various dances during three days of the Christmas period, while others confined their festivities to Twelfth Night. It is obvious that the Black slaves followed the Christian calender of their masters although their dances celebrated their own religious rituals.

Another example of a purely Black ritual becoming associated with a Christian festival is the *Matar la Culebra*, or kill the snake dance, performed in Havana, Cuba, and recorded as late as 1951 by the Cuban scholar Fernando Ortiz. This was regularly performed on Twelfth Night or the Day of Kings festival. A large group, sometimes referred to as a 'mob', of Black dancers paraded through the streets, dancing and singing, one section carrying on their shoulders a huge representation of a snake or ophidian. References in the songs to the terrible characteristics of the snake preceded the ritual killing of the serpent, after which the crowd danced in celebration around the dead creature. The snake being a well-known religious – and sometimes sacred – symbol amongst Black West Indians, often appearing in Voodoo and Nañingo ceremonies, this is a ceremony that has been passed down since the earliest days of the slave trade in the sixteenth century. Unfortunately there appear to be no descriptions of the actual dances themselves.

3

Sacred Dances

The curious gap in Black ritual dance celebrations occurs with wedding dances or rather, the lack of them. Insofar as there were no formal or legal marriage ceremonies provided for the Black slaves on the plantations of the southern United States it is understandable; what few ceremonies existed in the British West Indies followed English customs. But one would expect that the West African slaves would have brought with them some relics, however changed or distorted, of the dances performed at some wedding ceremony. On the other hand, the tribes of West Africa were polygamous, the great kings of, for example, Dahomey having several hundred wives and even the poorest of their subjects having three or four. Thus wedding ceremonies would not be thought particularly important; the mating dances like the Calenda and Chica being sufficient to celebrate the union between man and woman.

By far the most important ceremonies which demanded dance as part of the ritual were those associated with death. The universal belief amongst West African tribes of a life after death, in which the soul of the dead person may remain within his earthly habitat, or if disturbed or unhappy, roam at will causing much trouble, occasioned many elaborate incantatory dances. These were known on the coast of West Africa as Tovodoun and exported to the West Indies as the Voodoo ceremonies of Haiti, the Shango rites of Trinidad, the Obeah of Jamaica and the Nañingo of Cuba.

The religions and beliefs of the West African tribes varied from kingdom to kingdom, village to village, but there were three basic principles which affected the distribution of ritual throughout the Caribbean: one, the religion was a part of everyday life as regular in its observance as eating, not the weekly visit to church as with Christian communities; two, the religious practices included elaborate ritual; and three, these rituals involved much dancing.

The ultimate religious experience was to be possessed by a god, and this state of possession was induced by drumming and dancing. Many, though not all, of the dancers at a religious ceremony would become 'possessed' by the spirit of the *loa* or god – and this 'possession' was often aided by the consumption of alcoholic spirits. Possession usually resulted in a state of extreme physical frenzy, often likened by Western observers to an epileptic fit.

Of the many religious dances practised throughout the Caribbean it has been the Voodoo rituals of Haiti that have occasioned most comment and much misreporting of a sensational nature, including black magic, sorcery, human sacrifice and cannibalism. In reality, however, the Voodoo dances were more often performed in honour of an ancestor, or to expiate some unintended insult to a dead person, or to perpetuate his memory and retain his spirit in its familiar habitat.

The styles of dance vary tremendously but one particular movement, the rapid shaking of the shoulders, would seem to be common to all of them. One of the dances, the Zepaule, takes its name from the French word meaning 'shoulder'. Writing of another Haitian dance, the Danse

▼ *A print published in Paris in 1839 illustrating a Black funeral. Such occasions were often the scene of lively festivities, including dancing, to entertain the soul of the dead one on its journey.*

Nago, the anthropologist Alfred Metraux recorded: 'It is ... distinguished by its rapidity and violence. The steps are short and hurried, the pirouettes numerous, the shoulders seeming to be shaken by a continuous trembling accompanied by a certain swinging of the hips requiring an unbelievable muscular suppleness.'

At all these dance ceremonies it was, of course, the drums which provided the rhythmic impulse, the beat(s) rising and falling, usually gradually accelerating and rising in crescendo as the dancer(s) became more and more intoxicated with the steps, more and more possessed by the *loa*. The drums used for the Voodoo rituals were considered sacred; they were anointed in a separate ceremony and never used for any other purpose.

Shango was a cult similar to Voodoo, and took its name from the god of thunder worshipped by the West African Yoruba tribe. Following the slave trade, the cult persisted in Brazil, Cuba and Trinidad. As with Voodoo, the main object of the Shango ritual was to induce possession by one's god, and included many arcane routines and sacred objects specific to whichever personal god was being invoked. The dances themselves were notable for the lightness, skill and precision with which they were performed. Two American anthropologists, Melville J. Herskovits and Frances S. Herskovits, witnessed a Shango dance performed by a woman during the process of calling up the god Asharoko: 'The next one possessed was a woman, another "strong" dancer, who signalled for something which she described in gestures. A goblet with a green ribbon about its neck was brought to her, and this she placed on her head and began to dance. Without a headpad to steady it and without spilling any of its contents she danced vigorously for thirty-five minutes.' Vigorous it may have been but it was in considerable contrast to the many violent, contorted forms of dancing recorded at Voodoo ceremonies.

The cult of Obeah, practised in Jamaica, was a type of witchcraft emanating from the Ashanti tribe of West Africa and, like Voodoo, gathered around it a tremendous mythology of evil. It also included in its rituals a form of violent dancing that could continue all night, although the magical incantations had more to do with the brewing of poisons and the harming of an individual through fear than calling up of personal gods. There seem to be no records of the actual forms that the dances took.

Nañingo, a Cuban dance cult, was also related to Voodoo and Shango, and drew its rituals from Yoruban rites, with specific worship of the sun in a dance called Diablito (little devil). These dances were described as 'convulsive' and 'joyous', and once again the executant

 An illustration by E. W. Kemble in the Century Magazine, *circa 1886, showing a voodoo ritual. Such occasions were usually kept secret and one wonders how the artist obtained access to it. Note the fetish objects on the ground.*

would be possessed or 'mounted' by the god or saint that he had called up with his dancing and the ceremonies and fetishes that accompanied it.

Elaborate rites attended the funerals of West Indian Blacks. Although the dances were often expressive of sorrow at the loss of the departed, they also accentuated a feeling of joy so that the soul of the dead one should be entertained on its journey. There was also a strong sexual connotation in many of the dances, the eroticism serving both as an emotional release and reaffirmation of the life force in the midst of death. Katherine Dunham, anthropologist, dancer, choreographer and teacher, recorded a funeral dance with sexual emphasis that she witnessed in Trinidad, a man and a woman surrounded by a circle of boys beating sticks together: 'The shuffle would take them clockwise, then, as if by mutual consent, they would shift into a pattern of low second position interrupted by cross-kicks with right and left leg alternately. Then they would shuffle again, and spurred by remarks from the sidelines, the center couple would come closer and the emphasis would move from the feet well into central torso, becoming unmistakeably sexual in intention.'

It is interesting to note how a properly trained dancer like Dunham makes a careful, professional description (the reference to 'second position') of the dancing, rather than relying on vague adjectives such as 'vigorous' or 'erotic', although the 'central torso' is probably a euphemism for the genital region.

Insofar as the life of a slave in the Caribbean and the southern states of America could hardly be thought a happy one, it was natural that death would be looked upon as a happy release, and those who mourned the departed would also rejoice at the end of an earthly burden. One observer, writing at the beginning of the nineteenth century, recorded that a slave funeral was carried out: 'Not with the afflicting solemnity of Christian rites, but with all the mirthful ceremonies of African burial, forming a scene of gaiety, which consists of music, dancing, singing and loud noise.' One is reminded, however, that the Irish, while practising Christian rites, can turn a wake into a merry occasion.

4

Plantation Dances

In the early eighteenth century the Black slave population of the southern states of America had grown considerably and in view of the harsh conditions under which they lived there were a number of insurrections and uprisings, the so-called 'Cato Conspiracy' which occurred on a plantation at Stono, some twenty miles west of Charleston, South Carolina, being the most serious. The slaves killed two guards in a warehouse, secured arms and ammunition and, joined by other Black slaves, proceeded towards Florida. This led to strict laws in South Carolina which were intended to prevent any such recurrence, and these laws were rapidly copied by other states.

The Stono insurrectionists had marched to the sound of drums, so Blacks were forbidden the use of any form of drum. This led to the improvisation of drum substitutes, such as cow hides stretched over cheese boxes as a form of tambourine, and cow bones knocked together as primitive percussive instruments. Thus the tambourine and bones became a traditional combination later incorporated into minstrel shows in which popular characters took the names of their instruments, Mr Tambo and Brother Bones.

Whistles were made from bark and reeds and the slaves revealed all manner of ingenuity in order to provide music and rhythm for their dances. Certain slave owners would make up a small primitive 'orchestra' from their slaves and even bought them banjos and fiddles so that they could entertain the white folks. But this was comparatively rare and the slaves usually had to improvise instruments for their own entertainment.

Vague references to certain dances performed by plantation Blacks sound very much like variations on the Chica, and it was not uncommon for the best and most proficient of the Black dancers to be called to the 'Big House' to perform their dances (they were also adept at picking up the white folks' dances, such as jigs and reels). Solo dances performed by the men were often referred to as the Buck. Another favourite was the Pigeon Wing sometimes also referred to as the Chicken Wing. In both dances the performer would ape the manner of a courting pigeon or cockerel, strutting around, holding his arms bent close to his sides like wings. When the two types of dance were performed together it gave rise to the term Buck and Wing. It was mostly the men who performed the dances, particularly the Buck, but women were also frequent performers when the Pigeon Wing became an obvious mating dance. Both the Buck and the Pigeon Wing appear to have been performed over a wide area of the southern states, from South Carolina to Indiana, Mississippi to Texas.

In West African tribal dances there appear a number of movements imitating animals, birds and reptiles: camels, lions and panthers, cockerels and buzzards, lizards and snakes, even fish. To a lesser extent the imitation of North American animals and birds occurred in many of the early plantation dances invented by the slaves.

▼ *An illustration dated 1852 showing Black plantation workers dancing in the grounds of the 'big house'. Note the seated figure, second from left, making percussive rhythm with a set of bones.*

▲ *A late eighteenth-century American water-colour showing Black plantation workers enjoying a dance in their quarters.*

One of the most popular dances on the plantations was the Buzzard Lope. Its fairly elaborate pantomime – accompanied by descriptive doggerel – enacted the walk and pecking movements of a buzzard feeding off carrion, and descriptions by former slaves of having seen it performed tallied in many respects with that of a dance performed by the natives of Dahomey in West Africa.

Another popular dance, one which remained with the plantation slaves much longer than the Buzzard Lope and which eventually made the transition into minstrel shows, was the Cake Walk. It was essentially a competitive dance for couples and is interesting inasmuch as it is closer to European dance forms than African tribal dances. In fact it may have been a Black emulation of the minuet. The Cake Walk began as a dance called the Chalk Line Walk. One elderly plantation worker recalled the dance in these terms: 'The Cake Walk, in that section and at that time, was known as the Chalk Line Walk. There was no prancing, just a straight walk on a patch made by turns and so forth, along which the dancers made their way with a pail of water on their heads. The couple

▲ *A woodcut illustrating a pre-Civil War Saturday night dance by Black plantation workers. Despite the tendency of the artist to caricature the characters, he has captured the uninhibited gaiety of the occasion.*

that was the most erect and spilled the least or no water at all was the winner.' Later the pail of water seems to have been abandoned and the Cake Walk became a dance of some elegance. It was customary to perform it at the end of harvest or crop-over when the plantation owner would offer a prize of a cake to the best couple. This took place sometimes in the yards of the slave quarters, sometimes in front of the verandahs of the Big House where the plantation owner and his family could witness the proceedings. It was all part of the dance festivals held to celebrate the bringing in of the harvest. If the dances were held in the slave quarters the Cake Walk would be but a small part of the occasion – and the most circumspect. There would be other, more vivacious dances, with singing and drinking far into the night.

Another dance which occurred far and wide across the southern plantations and which had its origin in West African religious ceremonies was the Ring Dance or Ring Shout. It had certain affinities with the competitive Juba and consisted of a dance performed 'with the whole body – with hands, feet, belly and hips'. The dancers formed a ring and proceeded with a step that was half shuffle, half stamp, and much pelvic swaying. It is interesting to note that it survived partly by accident: the Baptist church forbade drumming and dancing which was considered too indecorous for religious worship. However, the definition of dancing included the 'crossing of the legs' and as the Ring Shout was performed to hand-clapping and with a shuffling step it was deemed permissible. It is ironic that the church authorities should proscribe movements in which the legs were crossed when, in some of the most 'pagan' Black dances, such as in the Shango cult, the belief was that anything crossed, including the legs, would keep the gods away.

Reference has already been made to the Juba being performed in Cuba and the Bahamas; in the plantations of the south it was also a popular secular dance, often referred to as 'patting Juba', as it was

▼ *This illustration by J. A. Elder depicts a domestic scene in Virginia, with two boys entertaining the family with dancing.*

frequently performed to clapping, stamping and patting of the arms, torso and thighs, as drumming was forbidden. The dance was often accompanied by doggerel verse in which the word Juba becomes anthropomorphised, for example: 'Juba dis and Juba dat, Juba kill a yaller cat. Juba up and Juba down, Juba runnin' all aroun'.'

Christian holidays, such as Easter and Christmas, were occasions when the slaves were not only allowed but encouraged to dance, just as they were at harvest festivals and other ceremonies. On these occasions the dancing was for the entertainment of the plantation owner and the slaves would be dressed in their 'Sunday best' – even perhaps have clothes bought for them by the plantation owner; especially if, as was frequently the custom, owners placed their slaves in wagered competition with each other.

But it was Saturday nights when most slaves were able to forget their everyday cares and woes in dancing, when most plantation owners would allow them to indulge in 'frolics' (as long as they were far enough away from the Big House), which included a number of dances which might have appeared 'indecorous', to say the least, had they been performed in front of white folks. On these occasions the slaves would not only perform dances remembered from their tribal heritage but the older ones amongst them would take pleasure in 'talking about Africa.'

5

New Orleans

The city of New Orleans presents a unique spectacle of dance throughout the nineteenth century. The city was founded by French Canadians in 1718, together with immigrants from France. The city changed to Spanish rule in 1762, the occupation lasting until 1800, during which time there were migrations of Spanish-speaking peoples from the West Indies and Haiti, although the main influence remained French.

With the Franco-Spanish occupation the dominant religion was Roman Catholicism which was fairly tolerant of Black dance and Negro customs. There was also a close commercial association between the state of Louisiana and the West Indies. French ships stopping at New Orleans also called at other colonial ports in Martinique, Guadeloupe and Haiti. Under the Spanish occupation the government was administered from Spain via Havana. These links with the West Indies and the European mainland directly affected the social and cultural development of New Orleans. When the French army of occupation in Haiti was defeated in 1803, Napoleon decided to sell the whole of Louisiana to the United States, a transaction that was known as 'the Louisiana Purchase'. Thus New Orleans became a melting-pot of cultures, a polyglot of immigrants where Afro-Caribbean Voodoo met European religion, where slaves dancing the Calenda, the Chica and the Juba met white aristocrats dancing the minuet, the waltz and the polka.

It was a commonplace for white men in New Orleans to take Black mistresses, despite a *code noir* issued from Versailles that forbade intermarriage or concubinage. The many offspring of these unions, known as 'mulattos', rarely became slaves because it was customary when a white man had a child by a Negro slave for the mother to be set free; the child was therefore automatically freed. Under the *code noir* these free mulattos could not marry either slaves or whites; the alternative for a woman was, again, to become the mistress of a white man. This commonplace choice produced an uncommon social phenomenon: the Quadroon Ball.

A quadroon was one quarter Negro, the offspring of a mulatto mother and a white father. Their skins were 'almost entirely white' and their features indistinguishable from the Creoles – children of European parentage born in the country. Although many of them had black hair and eyes it became increasingly common for a number of them to have fair colouring. There developed a very complicated class – or, rather, caste system – with the Creoles maintaining a distance between themselves and the quadroons who, in turn, were prejudiced against the mulattos who affected superiority over the slave Negroes. Even the slaves had their hierarchy: a Negro servant in one of the Big Houses being considerably 'above' a plantation worker.

It was usual for a quadroon woman to be 'presented' to a white

▶ *'The Love Song',
drawn by the author after
an original sketch drawn
from life in Congo Square,
New Orleans, which
appeared in the* Century
Magazine *in 1886.*

'A Negro Ball', Charleston, drawn by Eyre Crowe, in his book With Thackeray in America, *1893.*

► *'A Negro Ball', Charleston, drawn by Eyre Crowe, in his book* With Thackeray in America, *1893.*

man at the Quadroon Balls which were considered to be one of the sights of New Orleans; distinguished and even aristocratic visitors being taken there by their hosts. Originally organised by quadroon women as a means of presenting themselves and their daughters to white suitors, they were subsequently professionally promoted and a higher admission price was charged. Only upper-class white men were admitted; lower-class whites and mulattos were kept out, the quadroon women preferring an extra-marital affair with a white man to marriage with a mulatto. Such balls were held in the Condé Street Ballroom and, later, around 1810, in the new St Phillip Theater. Later still, in the 1830s, they moved yet again to the Orleans Ballroom. The events were regularly advertised in the local press.

Not surprisingly the dances at these Quadroon Balls were those of white society, many of the quadroons having been educated in Paris. On frequent occasions a white masked ball would be held on the same date as a Quadroon Ball when, after an appearance at the masked ball, several of the white males would hurry to the quadroon reception.

The mulattos and Negroes in the Big Houses, denied entrance to the Quadroon Balls, would imitate the whites' dances at their own gatherings. One domestic worker in a Big House recalled: 'Us slaves watched white folks' parties where the guests danced a minuet and then a grand march. . . . Then we'd do it, too, but we used to mock 'em, every step.' No doubt there was often a degree of mockery, but there were occasions when the emulation was also serious.

▲ *A drawing by E. W. Kemble, regular illustrator for the* Century Magazine, *showing a couple performing the Baraboula in New Orleans.*

In direct contrast to the conscious elegance and refinement of the Quadroon Balls were the black dances held to the north of the city in an area known as Congo Plains, more often referred to as Congo Square. These came about mainly through legislation enacted by the New Orleans City Council in 1817. During the slave revolt in Haiti in 1803 there had been a large influx of refugee plantation owners and their slaves who had sought refuge in New Orleans. Many of the slaves were devotees of Voodoo and they continued the practice within several 'secret societies' in the city. The whites became very nervous about these clandestine meetings which spread with some rapidity amongst the immigrant slaves, thus provoking the ordinance which stated:

> The assemblies of slaves for the purpose of dancing or other merriment, shall take place only on Sundays, and solely in such open or public places as shall be appointed by the Mayor, and no such assembly shall continue later than sunset, and all slaves who shall be found assembled together on any other day than Sunday, or who, even on that day, shall continue their dances after sunset, shall be taken up by the officers of police, constables, watchmen or other white persons, and shall be lodged in the public jail, where they shall receive from ten to twenty-five lashes.

It may seem strange that the City Council appointed the Lord's Day as the one on which the slaves should be free to pursue their 'dancing and merrymaking' but of course they were working at all other times; to allow such licence during working hours would invite a relaxation . against the laws pertaining to the God of Mammon.

It is most unlikely that Voodoo-dancing was performed in Congo Square, although one observer reported seeing dances in a nearby abandoned brickyard, a 'well-known Voodoo meeting place'. Voodoo rites were essentially secret, never open to the public gaze.

Sunday dances had been held in Congo Square some time before the City Council's legislation, just as any open space or common land anywhere was likely to become the venue for various forms of entertainment. Indeed, Congo Square was the location not only for dancing, but for dog-fights, cock-fights, bull-fights and various ballgames such as *raquette*.

From all accounts the dances that the slaves enjoyed were the Chica, Bamboula, Calenda and Juba, those familiar favourites which had been established throughout the Caribbean in various forms. Yet again their performance brought forth uncomprehending and derogatory epithets from the white observers who referred to them as 'brutally savage', 'dull and stupid', and the 'postures and movements' as resembling those of monkeys. A guide to the city of New Orleans referred to Congo Square as a place where 'Negroes dance, carouse and debauch on the Sabbath'. Naturally, dances such as the Calenda and the Chica would not appear to the white observer as having the style and elegance of those in the salons of upper-class New Orleans society, nor did any of those observers apparently have the wit or perception to see that they belonged to a totally different culture within which the dances had far greater significance.

Notwithstanding the generally expressed disapproval of the dances performed in Congo Square, a more tolerant attitude towards the 'Black debauchery' seems gradually to have developed by the middle of the century. An article in the *New Orleans Daily Picayune* in 1846 refers to the activities as 'novel, interesting and highly amusing', and, just as visitors to New Orleans were frequently taken to the Quadroon Balls, so a visit to Congo Square became part of the itinerary of every tourist.

It is ironic that after the Civil War, during which slavery was abolished, the interaction between Blacks and whites – not least in the dances they performed – decreased. The sharply defined caste system of the north was adopted by the very city where whites, Creoles, mulattos and slave Blacks had enjoyed a certain degree of freedom to mix (the various ordinances forbidding Blacks to attend Quadroon Balls were rarely observed). Many of the 'freed' slaves began to migrate north and the unique quality of life in New Orleans began to fade.

6

Dance on the Levee

▼ *A lithograph, dated 1878, showing Black roustabouts dancing on the levee, the banks and wharves of the Mississippi. Note the portable board placed on the bales of cotton.*

It was common practice for plantation owners who had no immediate use for their slaves to hire them out for a variety of jobs. Some of the slaves were semi-skilled and were 'on lease' as carpenters, blacksmiths, builders and even gardeners; more often they were hired as labourers and many of them worked as stevedores or roustabouts on the levee or banks of the great Mississippi river which wound through a large number of the plantations of the southern states. Others worked on board the huge stern-paddlewheel boats that plied up and down the river.

Life on the levee was rough and tough; most of the ports visited by the stern-wheelers had big Negro areas and in these quarters a number of dance halls and 'honky-tonks' sprang up.

Many of the dances performed in these sleazy saloons were variations of popular white social dances – jigs, reels, quadrilles, cotillions, waltzes – but the slaves also danced their own measures, including those imported from the Caribbean, the ubiquitous Juba, the Calenda and the Chica. As with New Orleans, in the big cities bordering the Mississippi – Natchez, Memphis, St Louis – the Blacks and whites would intermingle in the honky-tonks and bordellos where the white dances, jigs and reels, would frequently break down into 'patting Juba'.

Even further north, on the Ohio river which eventually makes confluence with the Mississippi, a young Cincinnati reporter, Lafcadio Hearn, recorded dancers performing the quadrille and the Virginia reel which gradually became 'patting *Juba*'.

After the abolition of the slave laws following the Civil War, the south was invaded by 'carpetbaggers', a pejorative term used to describe a number of politicians who opportunistically acquired the Negroes' votes after their enfranchisement. They contributed to the Negroes drifting north in search of work and a supposedly freer social climate, taking with them their popular dances. From the southern states of Louisiana, Texas, Alabama, Arkansas, Georgia, North and South Carolina, Mississippi and Tennessee, the immigrants drifted into Missouri, Kentucky, Indiana, Virginia and New York to join their brothers who had, in smaller numbers, endured the slavery of preceding centuries.

In the north there was frequent mention of dances performed by Negro slaves. In New York there were accounts of Dutch burghers travelling in from the countryside to see Negroes dancing. Many of these dances took place in New York's Catherine Market where, after the day's business was concluded, the slaves would regularly celebrate by dancing, their efforts being rewarded by the onlookers. The slaves carried with them large boards, some six feet square, which served as portable dancing areas for the jigs and breakdowns which were the popular dance forms. Music – or rather, rhythm – was provided by various makeshift drums or by the usual method of patting various parts of the body, the thighs and torso, and hand-clapping.

Both in the city of New York, and in upstate New York, the Protestant Dutch celebration of Pentecost was known as 'Pinkster Day', a holiday when the Blacks performed their native Congo dances or, as local records referred to them, the 'double shuffle, heel-and-toe breakdowns'. Other observers describe dances that sound very much like the Calenda.

▲ *A photograph, taken in the American deep South during the early 1930s, showing the use of a portable board for breakdowns.*

This brief survey illustrates that from the beginning of the slave trade in the seventeenth century to the end of the nineteenth century, Black dance, with its roots in West African tribal customs, had spread across the whole of the Caribbean, from Cuba to Trinidad, from Haiti to Martinique, and through the southern, central and north eastern states of the North American continent.

During these centuries Black dance had intermingled with white social dances; it had been absorbed into the festivals of the Christian calender, while in many other areas it had retained its unique style and format, a form of movement based on multiple rhythms, with a fluidity and flexibility unmatched by any other dance vocabulary.

More interesting – and more important – than any of these anthropological aspects, however, was the fact that Afro-Caribbeans had discovered that they could earn money by presenting their deep-rooted instincts to express themselves in dance.

7

Jim Crow, Juba and the Minstrels

There is considerable irony in the fact that, as Blacks became progressively aware that it was possible to earn a little money performing their dances for white folks, whites had already pre-empted them by imitating Black dances. Even before the revolution of 1776 there were records of such efforts and by the turn of the century white actors and dancers in Black-face were gaining popularity.

The most famous – or perhaps, infamous – of these entertainers was a white actor, T. D. Rice, who, in the 1820s, performed a song-and-dance act in Black-face. There are several stories of how he had observed a lame Negro groom performing a dance which he then adapted to a doggerel ditty:

> Wheel about, turn about,
>   Do jus' so
> An' ebery time I turn about,
>   I jump Jim Crow.

▶ *An American lithograph songsheet cover, circa 1835, showing T. D. Rice performing his celebrated 'Jim Crow' dance.*

(opposite) Another songsheet cover illustrating the 'Jim Crow' song and dance.

No one has been able to define the dance with any authority, but it has been conjectured as a circling movement in the familiar flat-footed shuffle of Ring Dances, possibly mixed with the popular jig followed by a small, syncopated hop or jump. What is probably more important than the actual steps, which were no doubt something of a choreographic hybrid, is the posture during the performance, the bending of the torso, the swaying of the hips and pelvis with the waving of the hands or the admonitory wagging of a finger.

Rice made a fortune out of his impersonation of the old groom, performing his Black-face song-and-dance act throughout America, where both the song and the dance became a national craze, and also in London and Dublin. The name Jim Crow comes from the groom's Christian name and the surname of the man in whose livery stable he worked; it being a common practice for Negro servants to adopt the surname of their masters. Since then, of course, it has become synonymous with those Blacks who went along with the white stereotype of the Negro races, prepared to acquiesce in making Black characters either sentimentalised or ridiculed.

One genuine Black dancer, William Henry Lane, achieved similar fame to Rice and indeed his success was even greater inasmuch as he surmounted the general prejudice against Blacks. Adopting the name Juba – presumably from the popular Black dance of that title – his name was foremost amongst the minstrel shows that attained great popularity during the 1840s.

Juba was born a free man, coming from Providence, Rhode Island. According to the distinguished American writer on dance, Marian Hannah Winter, Juba was taught by a Negro jig-and-reel dancer, 'Uncle' Jim Lowe, and his early professional years were spent performing such dances in the low dives, dance halls and saloons of lower Manhattan in what was known as the Five Points District (today it is the intersection of Baxter, Worth and Park Streets). It was an area of brothels and rooming houses, mainly occupied by freed Negro slaves and poor Irish workers, so it is not surprising that the Irish jig became intermixed with the Negro dances. By 1845 Juba had become the most famous interpreter of this hybrid dance to which he added many improvisations of his own. His ability was such that when he joined a minstrel troupe, the Ethiopian Minstrels, he was given top billing with the four white minstrels in the show – the only Black artist of that time to achieve such prominence.

He was billed as 'Master Juba, the Greatest Dancer in the World'! His fame increased after a series of challenge dances with a white minstrel, Master John Diamond, who had appeared in P. T. Barnum's

▶ '*Master Juba*', *the stage name of William Henry Lane. He appeared in Charles Dickens'* American Notes *and had a great success at Vaux-hall Gardens, London, in 1848. This illustration appeared in the* Illustrated London News *of that year.*

shows as a dancer of 'Negro breakdowns'. The outcome of the first challenge dance, held at John Tryon's amphitheatre, was undecided; two more matches were arranged at the Chatham and Bowery Theatres, after which Juba was acknowledged as the winner and accorded the title 'King of All Dancers'. In 1846 he joined a new troupe, White's Serenaders, and two years later journeyed to London to appear with Pell's Ethiopian Serenaders at Vauxhall Gardens.

Charles Dickens had seen Juba at Five Points during his visit to America and, writing under the pseudonym Boz, had referred to him in his *American Notes*. Without mentioning him by name Dickens (as Boz) wrote:

> Single shuffle, double shuffle, cut and cross-cut: snapping his fingers, rolling his eyes, turning in his knees, presenting the backs of his legs in front, spinning about on his toes and heels like nothing but the man's fingers on the tambourine; dancing with two left legs, two right legs, two wooden legs, two wire legs, two spring legs – all sorts of legs and no legs – what is this to him? And in what walk of life, or dance of life, does man ever get such stimulating applause as thunders about him, when, having danced his partner off her feet, and himself too, he finishes by leaping gloriously on the bar counter, and calling for something to drink, with the chuckle of a million of counterfeit Jim Crows, in one inimitable sound?

Not the least interesting part of that brilliant, imaginative account is the reference to Jim Crow, showing how the name had become sufficiently universal for Dickens to assume his readers would be familiar with it.

Master Juba's life was as short as his fame was widespread: he died in 1852 while still in London.

It remains purely conjectural how much of Juba's dancing was based on Black dance forms. It is known that the jig and the reel were incorporated into his performances; just how many of his improvisations were based on the Juba, or the Calenda or any of the Ring Dances it is impossible to know, but no doubt many of the audience, while recognising the jigs and reels, would have imagined they were watching authentic Negro dance, and Dickens' reference to single and double shuffles would indicate that there were, in fact, a number of Afro-Caribbean movements employed.

Solo performers may or may not have incorporated movements from remembered Afro-Caribbean dances, naturally they accentuated those steps at which they were most adept; but the minstrel shows, as they developed during the 1840s, adopted a form which, consciously or not, was derived from traditional Ring Dances of Africa, with a solo performer in the middle encircled by those who either sang or chanted an accompanying song and provided the rhythm with drums or hand-clapping.

For the purposes of stage presentation the circle was cut into a semi-circle facing the audience. The tribal ring-leader was transposed into a master of ceremonies and those providing the rhythmic accompaniment – Mr Tambo and Brother Bones – were seated at each end. The

▲ *Another scene from Dickens'* American Notes, *of Black dancers performing an exuberant breakdown in a bar room.*

first minstrels were all white, the first group being the Virginia Minstrels who included Dan Emmett who was the composer of the great hit song 'Dixie'. After the Civil War and the emancipation of the slaves, Blacks began to be included.

After the middle of the century the formula for such shows was fairly fixed, resolving into a three-part performance. The first part began with a certain amount of question-and-answer banter between the central interlocutor or Master of Ceremonies and the end-men, Mr Tambo and Brother Bones. After this comic interlude there would be some sentimental songs – vide 'Dixie' – followed by a Walk Around, a kind of grand promenade for the whole company.

The second part was the Olio which included singing, dancing and possibly verse-speaking, somewhat similar to any music hall format of later Victorian times. The final Afterpiece was performed once more by the whole cast and often included a burlesque of a popular drama.

The Walk Around – sometimes performed as a finale as well – was developed from the Afro-Caribbean Ring Dance and the Juba. For sixteen bars or so the whole company would shuffle around in a circle; then one of the dancers would enter the centre of the ring and perform a Juba solo which was more readily known as a breakdown. When six dancers or soloists had all shown their paces they came downstage and danced together while the rest of the company patted time, or clapped hands and shuffled.

During this time a dance evolved that was directly developed from Negro dance movement. Called the Essence of Old Virginia, the step was derived from the Black dancers' use of an intricate shuffling step, a heel-and-toe movement that produced an effect of gliding across the floor. Originally performed in quick-time, it was perfected by a Black-face minstrel, Dan Bryant, who executed it quite slowly. It is one of the few genuine Black dance movements that were incorporated by professional minstrels, and may perhaps have been the origin of what was later to be known as the Soft-shoe Shuffle.

The white professionals who performed in Black-face created a grotesque stereotype, a caricature of Negro features and characteristics that, within two decades, had become so indelibly fixed in the public's eye that it has persisted to this day. Black-face minstrels danced and sang; *ergo*, all Negroes danced and sang. Black-face minstrels were funny with their large, painted-on mouths, their rolling eyes and their shock-wigs; *ergo* all Black people looked and behaved in a comic manner. This bizarre image persisted deep into this century and certainly no minstrel group, whether Black-face or genuine Negro, would have tried to present any other, more natural, impression. In fact, when genuine Negro minstrels were formed, many of them actually made their faces darker and encircled their mouths with white make-up to increase them to twice their normal size.

Yet while with hindsight one deplores such a mass misrepresentation of racial characteristics – and the prejudice it helped to engender – the emergence of so many talented Black performers brought a new vitality to many aspects of professional dancing and a revelation of what Negro dance had to offer on the American stage. The Afro-Caribbean dances, the rhythmic precision, the intriguing stop-time effects, created a base from which far more sophisticated entertainment and entertainers were to emerge.

8

Late Minstrelsy and the Soft-Shoe shuffle

The Soft-shoe Shuffle was the opposite to those dances originating from the Irish jig and the Lancashire clog dance which had been adopted by the Black and white minstrels and transformed into something masquerading as Negro plantation dances. The Soft-shoe Shuffle was much closer to the genuine thing – which was quite likely anyway to have been performed barefoot – and much more elegant in execution.

While performing the jigs and clog dances the body was held erect with the arms kept straight and stiff at the sides and all the virtuosity concentrated in the feet. In the Soft-shoe Shuffle the rapid footwork was still there but often taken at a slower tempo. More importantly, perhaps, it allowed the torso to move with greater flexibility: that suppleness of the spine and rotatory looseness of the pelvis that is so inherent in Black dancers from their earliest forms of tribal dances. It allowed the dancer to adopt a relaxed, insouciant style that aided the development of a comic character and also left the dancer free to use his arms and hands for additional expressive movement, to accompany himself on tambourine, fiddle or banjo.

The Soft-shoe Shuffle was an ideal dance for the minstrel to portray the fallacious image of the simple, happy, indolent Negro servant and the dances were frequently accompanied by songs which reinforced such a stereotype.

The most famous exponent of the Soft-shoe Shuffle was in fact a white man called George Primrose who was born in 1852 and continued working well into the twentieth century. He was an Irish Canadian from London, Ontario, whose real name was Delaney. Despite the fact that he was white, he influenced many Black dancers of the time, often performing with Black minstrels and on the same bill with Negro vaudeville acts: an instance of Black dance being imitated, given a sophisticated polish and then handed back to its initial exponents.

Minstrelsy boomed after the end of the Civil War and received a tremendous new impetus after the first transcontinental railroad was completed in 1869. It was the Black-face minstrels who predominated although there were a number of genuine Black minstrels, and the shows began to ingest all sorts of other entertainment acts, such as Irish ballad singers and slapstick comedians.

One of the great exceptions was the Georgia Minstrels, created by a black man, Charles Hicks. It was one of the most famous troupes and the name was appropriated by a number of other companies trading on the success of Hicks' original. But Hicks encountered much colour prejudice which eventually forced him to sell the show to a white entrepreneur, Charles Callender, in 1872. Six years later it was bought by another white impresario, Jack Haverly, who changed the name to Haverly's European Minstrels and took the troupe on a successful foreign tour. Black artists continued to predominate and, among others of front rank, Haverly employed James Bland, the composer of 'Carry me back to old Virginny'. In those days it was the minstrel shows which were the main medium for creating popular song hits.

▼ *This poster advertising '40 whites and 30 blacks' shows how late minstrel shows grew to be big, spectacular entertainments.*

The small, intimate, comparatively simple minstrel show began to be swallowed up in ever larger and more spectacular entertainments. In 1882, an impresario named Gustave Froman produced the biggest minstrel spectacular of all, resurrecting the name of Callender and calling it Callender's Consolidated Spectacular Colored Minstrels. After three years, during which business was indifferent, the show was disbanded. By that time there were other 'spectaculars' on the road but towards the end of the century the minstrel shows, both Black-face and Negro, were in decline, and vaudeville was beginning to take over.

The life of the Negro minstrel was often a precarious and dangerous one, the high profile of the Negro as an entertainer marking him out as a target for all sorts of violence, especially in the south where most Blacks were content to conform to the docile servant role. In their book *Jazz Dance* Marshall and Jean Stearns quote a Black minstrel musician, W. C. Handy, as enduring some 'searing experiences': for example, a colleague was lynched in Missouri; while in Orange, Texas, local cowboys riddled the minstrels' car with bullets. In another Texas town, where a member of the troupe contracted smallpox, the local doctor seriously suggested lynching the whole company as a protective measure.

Small, unpretentious minstrel shows struggled on for a few years into the new century but the swollen spectaculars were symptomatic of a dying form. Minstrel shows were, of course, entirely male and the appearance of women in vaudeville, together with new vernacular dances such as the Hoochy-Kootchy and the Shimmy – albeit deriving their movements from Afro-Caribbean origins – added the *coup de grace*. Simple, innocent fun was out, sexual sophistication was in.

9

Medicine Shows, Gillies and Carnivals

As the minstrel shows waned around the turn of the century, so medicine shows, gillies and carnivals became more popular, a kind of adjunct to the minstrels, less 'pure', more razzmatazz, the bottom end of show business with all the attendant vicissitudes: the financial precariousness, the charges of vagrancy, the attention of pimps and social parasites.

Even so, they were a useful, if very rough and ready, schooling for the young Black who wanted to break into the entertainment industry. If you could attract a crowd, strut your stuff and make a few dollars while working for a medicine show, you could handle the most demanding of audiences. It was the proving ground for a number of highly talented Black dancers, singers and musicians who went on to comparatively great things in later years.

Most medicine shows consisted of a wagon equipped with bunks and a portable stove; it was run by a 'doctor' aided by two or three assistants who, besides drumming up a crowd with their singing, dancing and clowning antics, went amongst the customers selling all manner of unspeakable lotions, potions and ointments 'guaranteed' to cure everything from constipation to consumption.

The wagons would stop on the outskirts of small towns, or even dare to invade the big cities. The dancers would do their turn right there on the sidewalk – probably keeping an eye open for the patrolling policeman – then the 'snake oil', or salt mixed with Coca Cola, or turpentine and molasses, or whatever lethal concoction it was, would be quickly sold from the back of the wagon with such sales guff as 'Only six bottles left!' or – to some dubious customers – 'Be patient, ladies and gentlemen, you'll all get your bottle!'

The dances ranged from the Buck and Wing, the Strut, the Soft-shoe Shuffle, jigs, reels, jumps, twists, and any step or acrobatic manoeuvre the executant could do best. Sometimes they accompanied themselves on the tambourine or banjo, sometimes the music or rhythm was provided by a colleague.

If medicine shows were just about the nadir for any dancer who wished to be considered a professional, then gillies were the next step up the ladder. A gillie – named after the wagons which accommodated and transported the equipment – was a kind of small travelling fair. There would be one or two mechanical rides, a carousel, a switchback even, perhaps a small ferris wheel, side-shows, tents to accommodate hula girls and 'freaks', maybe a fortune-teller and a shooting gallery or Aunt Sally. Amongst it all – and the only Black faces amongst this hotch-potch of entertainers – would be the dancers in their own little tent. Outside there was a small collapsible stage where the performers – dancers, musicians and acrobats – would be called out by the barker to give the crowd a taste of the excitements they could expect inside the tent. The dancers would go into their wildest routines, their most frantic jigs and reels, their liveliest breakdowns, twists and turns to inveigle the customers in. Within the tent, a rope separated Blacks from whites in the audience.

The show usually began with a comedian cracking jokes – working in local references like any music hall comedian, interrupted by special-ity acts such as jugglers or acrobats and some eccentric dancing. There would be some ensemble work with the company singing and dancing together with, perhaps, a special 'spot' for a musician, and the show would close with an Afterpiece, a favourite sketch and dance number affectionately known as Eph and Dinah.

► *A poster advertising Black troubadours in a buck-dancing contest as part of a vaudeville show.*

Eph and Dinah would be two dancers dressed up as quaint old folks on a plantation. On would come Young Rastus who, with jokes, asides and pantomime would work up some simple plot such as revealing it was the old folks' wedding anniversary. The assembled company would encourage them to dance whereupon Eph would do a few doddery steps and sink down exhausted. Then Dinah would do the same. Egged on by Rastus, Eph would essay something a little more energetic, say the Turkey Trot or the Possum Walk, similar to those popular plantation dances the Pigeon Wing and the Buzzard Lope. To the audience's surprise and delight Eph would grab hold of Dinah who would also reveal herself as a spritely party and the two of them do the Slow Drag with bumps and grinds and many a lascivious wink and whoop, ending with some really virtuoso steps and acrobatics.

Dances in the Jig Top, as the tent was called, often made use of the two stereotype Black characters, the slow-witted, shambling, plantation hick and the city dude, flashily dressed with curly-brimmed hat or boater, silver-knobbed cane and patent shoes, a fast-talking street-smart dandy who scored over his country cousin. If these caricatures helped to fix a fallacious image of the Black race, if that image consolidated prejudice and ignorance, it also paved the way for other Black artists to go on to better things as entertainers; it provided a springboard for those whose ambitions were greater and whose awareness of the social injustices suffered by the Blacks developed in tandem with their acceptance as artists.

A gillie helped the individual dancer towards that acceptance; it enabled him to work on a routine, to portray character through the dances he chose to perform or even create and to start to build a career. It was an important step towards the 'big-time'.

Carnivals were the next step up. Not dissimilar to gillies the carnivals were larger and somewhat more stable as an organisation. They would probably include some animal acts as well as the rides and sideshows and often there was a band in attendance as well as the small group of instrumentalists who played for the dancers and minstrels. The whole troupe travelled by train rather than wagon.

While the plantation songs and dances were the staple fare of the dances, with the semi-circle of performers, the end-men and the master of ceremonies in the middle, the speciality dancers and the final Walk Around, it was the period of ragtime and the beginning of jazz – of a whole new exciting era when the black dancers, singers and musicians would establish themselves in the forefront of white theatre.

10

Transitions

As minstrelsy declined so Black artists began to be accepted more and more into various forms of theatre.

In Harriet Beecher Stowe's famous abolitionist play, *Uncle Tom's Cabin*, adapted from her novel and first produced in 1852, the Black characters were originally acted by white actors in Black-face; within a decade or two the roles were taken by Black actors and by the end of the century the drama had acquired all sorts of accretions: one production had a 'ballet' of Negro girls, another introduced the Cake Walk, while yet another, in 1892, had the actress playing Topsy performing several breakdowns!

The Cake Walk had by now become a popular dance far removed from its early, genuine, plantation days as a harvest festival or Saturday night competition dance. In 1889 an all-Negro show opened in New York called *The Creole Show*, in which the Cake Walk was one of the most popular items, presented as a splendid finale led by Charles Johnson and Miss Dora Dean, who were later married. Johnson was a clever, eccentric dancer who revivified the Cake Walk as a grand parade number, a strutting promenade which has been copied down the decades for many a similar burlesque, music hall or vaudeville finale. Dora Dean was the first Black woman to wear thousand-dollar dresses and the pair specialised in presenting themselves as a very elegant couple, continuing in vaudeville until the late 1930s.

The Cake Walk was also taken up as a popular dance form by whites, who performed it in ballrooms where Blacks were not permitted entrance.

Two years after *The Creole Show*, another production opened in New York, its title, *The South Before the War*, a direct invitation to white audiences to view a romanticised presentation of the deep south in all its 'glory'. It was an entertainment that made great use of plantation songs and dances including the Virginia Essence. In the chorus line was a twelve-year-old dancer who was later to become one of the most

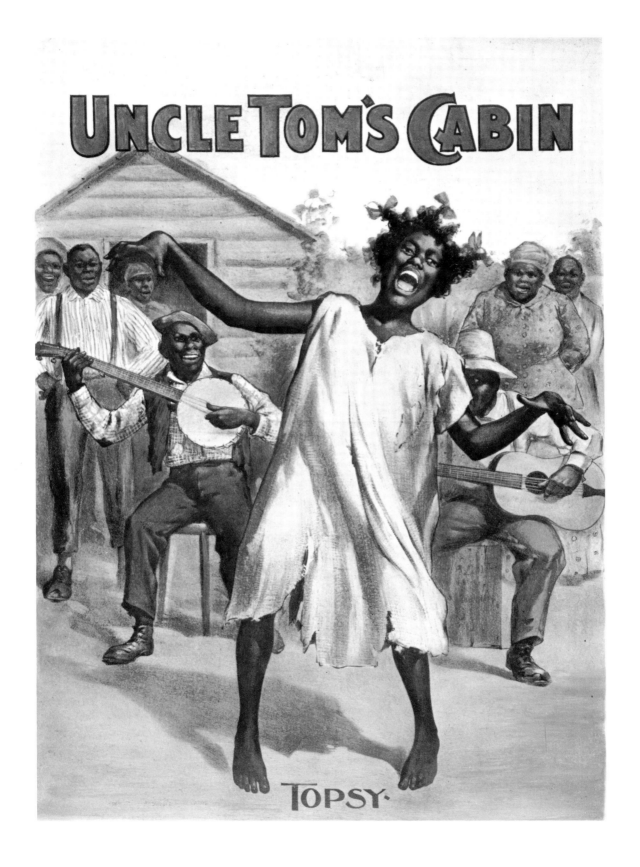

◄ *'Topsy', featured on a poster for a late nine-teenth-century stage adaptation of Harriet Beecher Stowe's* Uncle Tom's Cabin.

celebrated Black performers of all time, Bill Robinson. The show featured a chorus line of sixteen singing and dancing girls – a major departure for a show which still adhered to the format of the minstrel show. In line with this, the girls are supposed to have formed the usual semi-circle with a female interlocutor and male end-men.

In 1895 the Black agent for *The Creole Show*, John Isham, set up another, similar entertainment, *The Octoroons*. As before, it followed the minstrel formula with the show divided into the usual three parts and the Afterpiece or finale, including a Cake Walk, a military drill and a chorus march.

The following year Isham produced yet another all-Black show, *Oriental America*, the first all-Negro entertainment to open on Broadway. Although it retained the traditional three-part minstrel shape, the finale, instead of using the popular Cake Walk in the Afterpiece, substituted of all things a selection of operatic arias. Perhaps Isham thought that the 'serious' music was a necessary inclusion for Broadway audiences; whatever the reason, the show closed quite soon.

In 1898 came another all-Negro production which, in its complete abandonment of the minstrel format in favour of a progressive storyline, was a considerable step forward. Its title – which would be completely inadmissable today – was *A Trip to Coontown*. It was considered the first Negro musical-comedy, and was the first show to be completely performed, produced, directed and managed by Negroes.

Almost simultaneously another Negro musical, *Clorindy – the Origin of the Cake Walk*, opened after a long gestation period in which the first night was frequently postponed. The original intention was to star a great dancing and comedy team, Williams and Walker, but when the show was finally assembled they were out of town and another performer with minstrel experience, Ernest Hogan, took the lead. The show was an instant success and its composer-producer-conductor, Will Marion Cook, was the first musician to apply ragtime to a stage production with conspicuous triumph. Negro dancers, singers, actors and musicians had arrived in the heart of American theatreland.

Bert Williams and George Walker were a singing and dancing comedy team from the West Coast who finally made it in New York and became one of the most highly paid teams in the theatre. Walker was born in Lawrence, Kansas, and made his way to California working in medicine shows. He could sing, dance and play the tambourine and bones, and was the perfect example of how a Black artist could progress from the exigencies of the medicine show to the bright lights and high salaries of Broadway.

Williams and Walker were the great proponents of the classical

▲ *George Walker, Ada Overton Walker and Bert Williams in a scene from their production of* In Dahomey, 1903, *in which they tried to incorporate steps and movements they had seen performed by real Dahomean dancers.*

Negro comedy duo, the plantation hick and the city dude, with Walker the epitome of the high-stepping, strutting, flashily dressed man-about-town and Williams the slow, shambling, down-at-heel victim of Fortune. Their dancing reflected these characters exactly, Walker living up to his name with a stylish Cake Walk, Williams performing a shuffling dance sometimes called the Mooch. The pair also performed the Buck and Wing and between them they were credited with having done much to pave the way for other Black dancers to reach the top in entertainment.

Williams in particular, was considered to have touched many a nerve with his presentation of what a contemporary magazine article called 'the inner life and peculiar genius ... of the Negro'. Other observers felt that there was a sense of thwarted ambition about his persona: a feeling that the minstrel stereotype which he played to such perfection prevented him from ever becoming a serious actor; yet another instance, perhaps, of the clown wanting to play Hamlet. W. C. Fields referred to Williams as 'the funniest man I ever saw and the saddest man I ever knew'.

One brief but interesting episode in the career of Williams and Walker occurred before they left California for New York. During the San Francisco Winter Fair they saw some Dahomean dancers from the West Coast of Africa; they were so impressed by these people whose ancestors had filled so many slave ships that they tried to incorporate something of the Dahomean character into their shows with titles like *A Senegambian Carnival* and *In Dahomey*. However, after three or four centuries the manners and customs of the American Negro had become so far removed from those of West Africa and had been so overlaid with indigenous – if frequently fallacious – characteristics, that the elements of Dahomean culture had to be distorted in order to be incorporated in a way that audiences understood.

The Juba, the Buzzard Lope, the Pigeon Wing, the Possum Walk, the Buck and Wing, the Cake Walk, the Soft-shoe Shuffle, the Virginia Essence could – indeed in a few decades would – all be identified by anthropologists, but for the people in the stalls such dances came from the deep south or the Caribbean, not from Dahomey or Senegal.

11

The Cake Walk and Ragtime

Even though the minstrel shows went into decline towards the end of the nineteenth century, the Cake Walk remained as one of the most popular ingredients of transitional shows like *The South Before the War* and *The Creole Show*, and even appeared in Williams and Walker's attempt to introduce genuine tribal material in *In Dahomey*. Beginning as a West African tribal ceremony, the dance continued through the Afro-Caribbean Ring Shouts to plantation competition dances, and ended up as a dance craze that not only featured in Broadway shows but also in ballroom competitions across the world. Williams and Walker brought the Cake Walk to its ultimate development as a theatrical *tour de force*; and in its later manifestations they performed it to ragtime music, in itself another craze that swept the world.

The rhythmic complexity of West African drumming, the basis of so many of the dance rhythms that were brought to the Caribbean and the United States by the slave communities, harbours the seed of ragtime, whose chief characteristic is its effective use of syncopation. This syncopation – a displacement of either the beat or the normal accent of a piece of music, such as a short note on the first of the measure followed immediately by a longer note – was applied to any number of songs and tunes issuing from the music publishers of the time. These ragtime songs ranged from the boisterous 'Ev'rybody's doing it' to the near-blasphemous 'When ragtime Rosie ragged the rosary'. Irving Berlin's 'Alexander's Ragtime Band', composed in 1911, was probably the best known of all ragtime tunes – one that survived long after the cult of jazz had overtaken ragtime.

While the popular songs and ballads of the time – even old songs were subject to the syncopated style of ragtime – poured out of Tin Pan Alley, the centre for New York's music publishing, 'classic' ragtime was written for the piano by a number of musicians, many of whom were located in the mid-west, especially in the city of St Louis, and in the towns and cities bordering the Mississippi River.

▲ *The Cake Walk,*
which originated as a
competitive dance on the
plantations of the deep
South and became a
popular dance craze
throughout the world.

The greatest of these ragtime composers was undoubtedly Scott Joplin, born in Texarkana, Texas, only three years after the abolition of slavery. Joplin's father had been a slave; he was also an accomplished violinist who frequently played at dances. Joplin's mother sang and was an expert on the banjo so it is not surprising that at the age of eleven Joplin junior was considered something of a musical prodigy who received free piano lessons from a local German teacher.

At the tender age of fourteen Joplin left home, wandering through the raffish boom-towns of the mid-west and the south-east and earning his living by playing the piano in the saloons and bar-parlours that abounded in those regions. In 1895 he settled in Sedalia in Missouri and attended the George R. Smith College for Negroes run by the Methodist church, where he studied harmony and composition. These studies paid off when, four years later, he published the 'Maple Leaf Rag' named after the Maple Leaf Cafe of dubious reputation where he had been the regular pianist. The 'Maple Leaf Rag' sold over a million copies, the first great instrumental sheet-music hit in America, and it

meant that Joplin could give up his piano-playing and concentrate on composition.

In 1910 Joplin had composed the 'Stop-time Rag' which included the device of suddenly stopping the music while the dancers would fill in the silence with the sounds of their feet on the floor: tapping out the rhythm or sliding over the boards for a bar or two. In the same year that he composed 'Maple Leaf Rag', Joplin also wrote *The Ragtime Dance*, a 'ballet' for theatre performance based on Negro social dance steps – the Slow Drag, Backstep Prance, Stop-time and, of course, the Cake Walk – with a singer who called the dance figures. Joplin rented the Woods Opera House in Sedalia for a single performance of this work, having orchestrated his own rags, but it failed to obtain any popular response. It is ironic that seventy-five years later Kenneth MacMillan used many Joplin rags, including the title work, for his immensely successful comedy ballet *Elite Syncopations*.

Even less successful than *The Ragtime Dance* were the two operas that Joplin composed, *A Guest of Honor*, in 1903, and *Treemonisha* which received a single performance in Harlem in 1915. Its lack of success was instrumental in contributing to the composer's mental disintegration and his untimely death in the Manhattan State Hospital in April 1917, the day that America entered World War I. It is no exaggeration to say that the ragtime era died with Joplin.

It is not recorded what particular rags Williams and Walker used for their sensational Cake Walks, but it is reasonable to assume that many of Joplin's rags featured in them. The dance and the music were natural concomitants, a fusion of Black movement and rhythm and white harmony and instrumentation.

Short as the ragtime era was, its influence – and that of the Cake Walk – spread much further than America. John Philip Sousa, famous composer of marches and a distinguished bandmaster, formed his own band which he took on a world tour from 1900 to 1904. He incorporated the Cake Walk and various ragtime compositions in the band's performances, using a drummer who could syncopate the rhythm of whatever tune was being played.

The influence of ragtime even spread to the work of 'serious' composers, most notably Claude Debussy who as early as 1908 had written the 'Golliwog's Cake Walk' and Igor Stravinsky who composed his 'Piano-Rag Music' in 1919. But by 1920 the world of popular music, and with it popular dance, had been taken over by a freer, improvisatory style: jazz had arrived and rapidly established what is arguably the greatest contribution by Black culture to the world of dance.

12

Jazz

It is often assumed that jazz emerged, fully armed, from one particular honky-tonk, barrelhouse or ballroom in New Orleans. No one can say just where or when it began, although it is certain that it burgeoned around the beginning of the twentieth century as an offshoot of ragtime, becoming stronger and more firmly rooted than that growth, centred in New Orleans and the other towns and settlements along the Mississippi delta.

Jazz grew in an organic, disparate manner in the south-east of America as the result of several musical syntheses, some of them with European origins, others directly attributable to Black culture. It was like some new organism made fertile by a happy combination of the socio-cultural climate, by temperament and temperature, by new developments in communications, spreading with the rapidity of a feverish epidemic from city to city, growing new forms, shapes and structures as it went. And as it grew it inspired new dance ideas which were to become ever more interesting and important over several decades. What *is* certain in an uncertain musicological history is that it could only have happened in America.

Jazz does not have any musical features that cannot be found in other musical forms; its distinguishing factor is a flexible rhythmic impetus with variously syncopated phrasing – its direct development from ragtime. In particular the 'breaks', or extemporised passages, form its most distinctive characteristic, with the melodic element the least important. Indeed, the melodies of jazz were frequently borrowed from many sources, including baroque and classical music; its free form gave it the ability to go on developing and it did so in almost as many ways as there were executants to perform it.

Just as St Louis and the smaller towns of the mid-west had been the centres of the ragtime movement, so New Orleans was the largest incubation area for jazz. At the time New Orleans was the largest port in the American south, a melting-pot of humanity that held within it a

▲ *An early New Orleans jazz ensemble at the turn of the century.*

large number of entertainment businesses feeding off the peripatetic masses working along the length of the great Mississippi waterway. As described in chapter 5, it was a city rich in cultural heritage, with music and dance ingrained in every element of Black and white society.

The New Orleans style of jazz is generally associated – at least in its early years – with small instrumental groups composed of a cornet or trumpet, a trombone, a clarinet, a banjo or guitar, a string-bass and a rhythm section. This classic formation was liable to many variations, from trios right up to the big bands of the thirties and forties when jazz had fragmented into many new forms. In New Orleans there were also parade bands, mainly specialised brass bands for such big occasions as the Mardi Gras. The smaller units usually performed in cafes, honky-tonks and, particularly, dance halls.

The jazz style of playing, with the opportunities it gave to virtuoso instrumentalists to improvise their 'breaks' or cadenzas (one is reminded of the cadenzas improvised in concertos of the classical period) made an immediate and obvious appeal to those who found their entertainment in dance halls; it appealed to both the professional dancer and the amateur who took the musician's 'break' or 'riff' as an opportunity to invent and display his own steps and prowess.

In its early days, jazz and its related activities were closely linked to many forms of popular dance, and the changing fashions on the dance floor frequently shaped many of its developments. It was only in its later years that jazz became an element for an intellectual exercise and a musical form for serious listening.

Just as jazz bands of various configurations played music for ballroom dancing, so professional dancers and groups of dancers found jazz 'combos' the ideal collaborative backing for their shows, and throughout the first four or five decades of this century there were many notable associations between bands and dancers, both soloists and groups. From the Charleston to the Black Bottom, from the Lindy Hop to Jitterbugging, jazz finally synthesised all the Afro-Caribbean dance styles into an important and exciting new dance form.

13

Dance Halls

The commercial success of the Cake Walk, both in amateur contests and within the context of professional shows, was a precursor of the novelty dances which swept the dance halls and ballrooms for several decades, from the early 1900s to the forties and beyond.

The black population of the south, mostly left to its own devices with regard to entertainment, continued to find relaxation and amusement in dancing, despite the antipathy of the church and secular authorities. Blacks created many popular dance styles which, in later years, were taken up by professionals and popularised in the north for white audiences and dance hall customers.

Despite the disapproval of civic leaders, segregated dance halls proliferated in the south. There also developed a phenomenon called jook houses, the word 'jook' coming from *dzugu*, meaning 'wicked' in the Gulla dialect of the African Bambera tribe. Jook houses were Black bawdy houses for drinking, dancing and gambling and it was in these establishments that many of the dances that subsequently became universally popular originated.

One such dance was the Black Bottom. The name came from a tough neighbourhood in Nashville, Tennessee, and the dance was in demand in jook houses a decade or more before it was popularised, first in sheet music with lyrics by songwriter Perry Bradford in 1919, and then, with different lyrics by three white composers, on Broadway in George White's *Scandals* of 1926. White had seen the dance in a previous show, *Dinah*, in Harlem in 1924, before incorporating it in its new guise in his own production. Thus a popular dance by Blacks, known all over the south, was progressively appropriated until it finally became a commercial hit in the theatre.

Perry Bradford was a Black songwriter who was adept at writing lyrics to a number of dances he saw in the south. He would include in the lyrics instructions on how to perform the dance and in this way many popular dances gained a new impetus through sheet music.

Bradford's lyrics for the Black Bottom in 1919 were:

> Hop down front and then you Doodle back,
> Mooch to your left and then you Mooch to the right
> Hands on your hips and do the Mess Around,
> Break a Leg until you're near the ground,
> Now that's the old Black Bottom dance.
>
> Now listen folks, open your ears,
> This rhythm you will hear –
> Charleston was on the afterbeat –
> Old Black Bottom will make you shake your feet,
> Believe me, it's a wow.
> Now learn this dance somehow
> Started in Georgia and it went to France
> It's got everybody in a trance
> It's a wing, that old Black Bottom dance.

Doodle meant 'slide', and Break a Leg was, naturally, a hobbling step. It is interesting to note, incidentally, how the notation for jazz dance and popular dances was limited to such vernacular phrases as Doodle, Mooch, Truck, the Mess Around, and so on.

The song's reference to the Charleston is another instance of a Black dance form that was regularly performed all over the south long before it was taken up and presented by a number of professionals whose promotion of it made it into a dance craze that was world-wide.

The Charleston was known to Black performers such as the veteran minstrel writer and producer Noble Sissle as early as 1905, when he learnt it in Savannah. James P. Johnson, a pianist, recalled that it was regularly used in cotillions in 1913. By 1919 a dancer called Billy Maxie was teaching it to movie stars in California, and in 1920 there were Charleston contests in ballrooms all over America.

Both the Black Bottom and the Charleston were considerably refined and diluted from the original dance movements they incorporated. As with many popular dances that derived from African tribal dances (the Charleston came from an Ashanti ancestor dance) they incorporated the thrusting and rotational movements of the pelvis which had obvious sexual connotations and which usually acquired epithets such as 'lewd', 'grotesque', 'disgusting' and 'obscene'. Both the Black Bottom and the Charleston were popular ballroom dances that found their way into the theatre with great success, but there were many other ballroom dances that began in Black jooks and honky-tonks that did not achieve the same popularity.

Another of Perry Bradford's dances with accompanying lyrics that gave the instructions as to how it should be performed was the Bullfrog Hop:

► *An American sheet music cover from the early 1920s illustrating a dance hall with a jazz band attraction.*

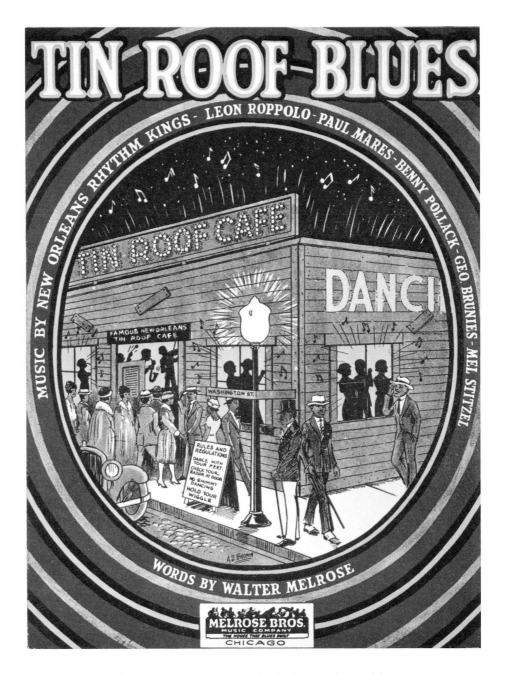

First you commence to wiggle from side to side
Get way back and do the Jazzbo' Glide
Then you do the Shimmy with plenty of pep
Stoop low, yeah Bo', and watch your step
Do the Seven Years Itch and the Possum Trot
Scratch the gravel in the vacant lot
Then you drop like Johnny on the Spot
That's the Bullfrog Hop.

As a dance it never achieved the popularity of the Black Bottom or the Charleston, but it is noteworthy in that its lyrics refer to other types of dance that were also very popular, and they also contain a prophetic reference to another movement which was to become a craze.

There were a whole series of animal dances which were introduced to ballroon dancers during the years from 1910 to America's entry into World War I in 1917, with titles such as the Turkey Trot, the Grizzly Bear, the Monkey Glide, the Chicken Scratch, the Bunny Hug, the Kangaroo Dip and – as referred to in the lyrics of the Bullfrog Hop – the Possum Trot. These were all novelty dances, many of which were reminiscent of the old plantation Buzzard Lope and Chicken Wing. The reference to the Shimmy was prophetic inasmuch as, although it was a movement long associated with Black dance, in particular many of the Haitian Voodoo dances with the rapid shaking or shimmying of shoulders and hips, it was later to be popularised by two white performers, Mae West and Gilda Gray, both of whom claimed to have invented it.

Mae West performed the movement in Arthur Hammerstein's show *Sometime* in 1919, and Gilda Gray did it in Ziegfeld's *Follies* of 1922. Once again it is an example of a Black dance movement being appropriated by white artists who proclaimed it as their own creation.

Another perennial favourite which had been danced by Blacks in the south years before it appeared in the Ziegfeld *Follies* of 1913, was Ballin' the Jack. The phrase comes from a railroad expression: 'the jack' was the common name for a locomotive, and 'ballin'' is a contraction of 'high balling', the trainsman or guard's signal to start moving. Thus 'ballin' the jack' meant to travel fast and, by inference, to have a good time.

Once again the original movements incorporated in the dance were considered unseemly, the rotation of the pelvis, sometimes called the Georgia Grind, being the offending action. The lyrics, as with so many dances of the period, contain the choreography:

> First you put your two knees close up tight
> Then you sway 'em to the left
> Then you sway 'em to the right
> Step around the floor kind of nice and light
> Then you twis' around and twis' around with all your might
> Stretch your lovin' arms straight out in space
> Then you do the Eagle Rock with style and grace
> Swing your foot way 'round then bring it back
> Now that's what I call Ballin' the Jack.

It was the 'twis' around' that caused the trouble, but it did not stop the dance becoming one of the favourites of all time, frequently revived

▶ *A songsheet of the Jelly Roll Blues by 'Jelly Roll' Morton, circa 1915. Black music, in the form of jazz, had by now invaded dance halls all over the world.*

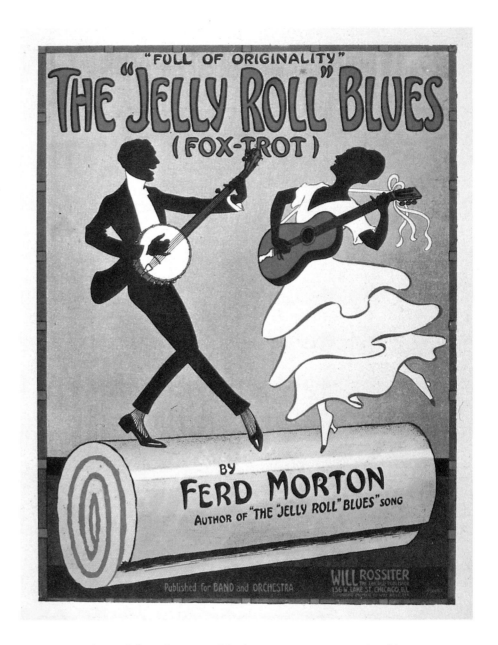

over a number of decades, notably by Danny Kaye in the fifties who at last gave it some social grace. Ballin' the Jack was a dance still being taught in the dance studios of California in the seventies.

The dance craze that lasted from the first decade of the century right through World War I and on into the twenties found most of its material in movements that could be traced back to the earliest dances brought to America by the slave population. Together with ragtime and jazz the Black influence had taken root both in the social dances of the time and in the big musical shows of Broadway.

14

Early Stars and Shows

Even though they helped to crystallise the image of the Black man as a comic grotesque, Williams and Walker also paved the way for Black artists to be accepted on Broadway and the major theatrical circuits across the country. Slowly the Jim Crow and Uncle Tom associations faded to be replaced with dancers capable of investing their performances with dynamic energy and virtuoso brilliance. Among the first to achieve this new radiance were The Whitman Sisters.

There were four actual Whitman sisters, Mabel, Essie, Alberta ('Bert'), and Alice, who joined the troupe some years after it had been established by her elder sisters. Their father was the Reverend Whitman who became a bishop of the Methodist church, first in Lawrence, Kansas, then in Atlanta, Georgia. At first Mabel and Essie helped to raise money for the church, singing harmony songs. In 1904 they were joined by Alberta in New Orleans where they established a company called The Whitman Sisters' New Orleans Troubadours. The troupe travelled all over the south ably managed by the formidable Mabel. When their mother died in 1909 the youngest sister, Alice, joined the troupe which also included a number of highly talented young Black dancers used as 'picks'. The word was short for 'pickaninny' which probably comes from the Portuguese word *pequenino*, meaning 'little one'. Picks were regularly used as backing for a show by white artists, singing and dancing with a unique combination of charm and talent – and of course they were very cheap, getting only a subsistence allowance. The Whitman Sisters had the pick of the picks because Black parents were assured that their young offspring would be well looked after.

Some of these young picks, such as Aaron Palmer, Samuel Reed, Julius Foxworth and Tommy Hawkins, became notable performers in their own right. They were in Mabel Whitman's own pick show, called *Mabel Whitman and the Dixie Boys*, which toured Europe and Australia as well as all over America, Mabel Whitman singing and the boys dancing everything from the Cake Walk to the Double Shuffle.

After Mabel's tour she was joined by her other sisters in a road show that was entitled simply *The Whitman Sisters*. It was a 'class' show that was booked on major theatrical circuits. Mabel soon retired from the stage, but remained as an impressive company manager, ruling her picks with a rod of iron; Essie was featured as a comedienne, doing a drunk act – something rather exceptional for a woman; Alberta did a male impersonation that was supposed to be the best of its day. Alice was billed as 'The Queen of the Taps', tap-dancing to many different

▶ *A photograph of Alberta 'Bert' Whitman, taken in 1928. Alberta regularly performed as a male impressionist.*

songs and tunes, and also doing Ballin' the Jack, Walkin' the Dog and the Shimmy. Alice married one of the original picks, Aaron Palmer, and their son Albert became the last member of the family to join the show, performing the Charleston in a tiny tuxedo at the age of four.

Little Albert or 'Pops' as he was nicknamed became one of the first acrobatic tap-dancers, doing the splits, cartwheels, and back-flips in his routine. Pops eventually left The Whitman Sisters and teamed up with a number of other young dancers, finally dancing with Louis Williams as a double act in which much of their material was extempory, doing whatever they felt like; both of them were able to play various musical instruments as well as dance.

Always on the lookout for new talent or a gimmick such as the baby Pops, The Whitman Sisters discovered a clever midget and adopted her, billing her as 'Princess Wee Wee'. Theirs was the best and most successful of all the Black vaudeville shows, with a cast numbering up to thirty, a chorus of twelve girls and a fine jazz ensemble. The show included speciality dance numbers, big production numbers with the chorus line doing high kicks, and Alberta and Alice doing a boy-girl song and dance, backed up by the chorus. When silent films became popular they shortened the show to fit in between screenings and continued to do good business. Mabel died in 1942 and the show continued for another year before finally closing. The Whitman Sisters provided an example to all other Black artists and were instrumental in furthering the careers of a large number of Black dancers.

One of the shows which established Black dancers on Broadway was *Darktown Follies* which was originally put together in Washington DC but opened in New York at the Lafayette Theater in Harlem in 1913. At the turn of the century the Black population of New York was centred around West 53rd Street, but by the end of the decade Black people had begun to trek north of Central Park to Harlem, which had been a white residential area. In 1913 the Lafayette Theater was integrated, along with a neighbouring theatre, the Lincoln, which also became popular with Black audiences.

The pioneering – not to say revolutionary – force behind *Darktown Follies* was John Leubrie Hill who helped write the book, composed the music, designed the sets and costumes and, having raised the money for the show, played the leading role of the virago of a wife!

The story concerned a wastrel who, having fallen in with bad company, mortgaged his father-in-law's plantation and went off to Washington DC hoping to get into high society and escape the retribution of his six-foot wife, Mandy Lee. Hill had previously worked with Williams and Walker and was a fine actor.

Darktown Follies included a number of dance routines, some familiar, some new, including a number called the Texas Tommy. The show closed with the usual Cake Walk but the big hit of the show was the finale of the second act with a Circle Dance for the whole company: a rhythmic sliding walk with each person's hands on the hips of the one in front. The company formed a continuous chain stretching across the footlights, round the back of the stage and joining up again in front, with a Mooch, a Slide and a Texas Tommy Wiggle, and singing Hill's song 'At the ball.... That's all'. The origin of the dance went back directly to the Ring Shout although the New York theatre critics imagined it was something that had happened spontaneously: there were no dance critics in those days and theatre critics had no idea of choreography as such, or how the steps of a dance might have originated.

Among the star dancers in *Darktown Follies* was Ethel Williams who would bring up the rear of the Circle Dance doing Ballin' the Jack; when the curtain came down she would put her hand round the side and continue to do the dance with her fingers, which brought the house down.

▼ *Clarence Robinson (left) with an unidentified member of the dance troupe he presented in Harlem during the twenties.*

In 1912 Ethel Williams had teamed up with a dancer called Johnny Peters, and the Texas Tommy had been one of their speciality dances which, like so many others, had been popular in the south before Black performers brought it north and incorporated it in shows. 'Tommy' was the vernacular for prostitute, and the wiggling hips and Georgia Grind were an essential part of the performance. It was very much a dance for couples, the girl dancing provocatively for the man; one of its characteristics was the separation of the couple, allowing each individual to improvise steps – a visual parallel to the jazz musician's 'break'. In this the Texas Tommy was a forerunner of the Lindy which emerged some fifteen years later and which was itself a precursor of the Jitterbug.

Another characteristic of the dance was that when the couples were together the girl would deliberately turn, slide or throw herself off balance, it being the job of her partner to prevent her from collapsing on the floor.

Johnny Peters is credited with introducing the Texas Tommy to audiences at Lew Purcell's, the only Black cabaret on San Francisco's Barbary Coast. Although Purcell's employed many Black artists, Blacks were not allowed amongst the audience.

Peters joined Al Jolson's troupe, partnering a dancer called Mary Dewson who fell ill when the troupe reached New York; Ethel Williams took her place. Peters and Williams appeared in many cabarets in and around the city, and also won a number of dance contests before being hired for *Darktown Follies*.

Within a few months of *Darktown Follies* opening at the Lafayette Theater, Florenz Ziegfeld had purchased the Circle Dance to incorporate in his own *Follies* on the roof of the New York Theater. The white artists, however, had some difficulty in performing the dance with the same panache as it had had at the Lafayette and Ethel Williams was sent for to help the cast, but was not asked to dance herself.

During the years from 1910 to 1917 Blacks hardly made an appearance on Broadway but white audiences began to make the pilgrimage uptown to Harlem, beginning a fashion that was to reach its height during the thirties and forties.

The big breakthrough came in 1921 when *Shuffle Along* was produced at the Sixty-Third Street Theater. The show was conceived by four talented Blacks, Flournoy Miller, Aubrey Lyles, Noble Sissle and Eubie Blake.

Lyles and Miller were dancers, actors, comedians and writers, who had both written for and acted with the Pekin Repertory Theater in Chicago; during their time in vaudeville their abilities were comparable to Williams and Walker who set the standard for so many Black artists.

Blake and Sissle were the musical team: Blake was a composer, conductor and pianist and Sissle was a singer and lyric writer. Between them this quartet had all the talents to create a successful musical comedy.

The plot of *Shuffle Along* concerned the election of a small-town mayor with the social pretensions of the contestants' wives as an added complication. The cast was assembled from artists who were personally known to the four creative producers, and they came from all over America.

The great difficulty – as always – was finding backers for the show; the breakthrough came when Harry Cort, son of a Broadway producer, was persuaded to take an interest. *Shuffle Along* was given a try-out in a Negro theatre, the Howard in Washington DC, and ran successfully for two weeks; it then moved on to another Negro theatre, the Dunbar in Philadelphia where Cort was persuaded to go and see it. In the company of a fellow producer, Abe Erlanger, he enjoyed the show immensely but was doubtful if it would appeal to white audiences. As a compromise they booked the show into a number of one-night stands in small Pennsylvania towns. The audiences were also small because no one had heard of the show, but it garnered rave reviews and armed with these Lyle, Miller, Blake and Sissle returned to New York. Cort was convinced that the show had popular appeal and found a derelict theatre on 63rd Street.

Off-Broadway was, in those days, also off the beaten track for theatre critics but one by one they came and gave the show enthusiastic reviews, although they were somewhat bemused as to what kind of show it was. Again and again they were complimentary about the dancing and the jazz score and there is no doubt that it was the vitality and inventiveness of the dancers that made *Shuffle Along* an eventual success.

Conversely, the show made several of the dancers into stars. Florence Mills, a singing and dancing specialist, was an immediate success, so much so that she was soon lured away by the offer of more money in another show with a Black emphasis, *Plantation Revue*.

Quite soon one of the chorus girls, hired as an end-girl, was causing something of a sensation by her comic antics: mugging, crossing her eyes, getting out of step, adding funny elaborations to the routine. Her name was Josephine Baker and she was destined to be one of the really big names in musicals and revue, an all-time great whose career became one of the most celebrated in the history of musical theatre.

The two male dancers originally featured were Charlie Davis and Tommy Woods. Davis specialised in the Buck and Wing, performing

▲ *Johnny Nit and Florence Mills in a dance duet* Shufflin' Home.

it with a speed, vitality and stamina that astonished the audience. Woods created a slow-motion acrobatic dance that was performed in perfect syncronisation with the music, including such tricks as the back-flip. Although acrobatic dancing was beginning to be known in cabaret it seemed new to the audiences of *Shuffle Along* and Wood's perfect timing was what gave his performance such élan.

Shuffle Along opened in New York in May 1921 and closed in August 1922, an unprecedented success for a Black show. Even so, theatre managers were deeply sceptical about whether it would appeal to audiences away from New York and there began another struggle to find theatres 'on the road'. Finally, the owner of the Selwyn Theater in Boston agreed to accept the show for two weeks during the height of the hot, humid summer. *Shuffle Along* filled the theatre every night for four months and only closed because of a threatened law suit from a Shakespearean actor, E. H. Southern, who had contracted to play at the theatre after the show's initial two-week run.

Despite the success in New York and Boston, theatre managers were still dubious; *Shuffle Along* had to travel all the way to Chicago for its next engagement, and that was in a broken down burlesque house, the Olympic. Despite the unsuitability of the venue – the view of the stage was badly obscured by a number of pillars – the show ran there for four months.

The next engagement was in Milwaukee, with the contract signed by the manager's assistant; when the manager returned to find out what had happened he left town in a rage, only to return once more to find his theatre with standing room only.

Similar success followed in Indianapolis, St Louis, Cincinnati, Pittsburgh, Philadelphia and Atlantic City; each time the theatre manager was sure that the show would not have the same success in *his* theatre, only to be confounded by the receipts.

When the show closed for the summer in June 1923, Miller and Lyles withdrew to work on another production, *Runnin' Wild*, their places taken by Lew Payton and the dancer Johnny Hudgins. Two other road companies continued with the show until 1924.

Shuffle Along had broken new ground for Black shows and had done much to conquer professional prejudice. Undoubtedly its greatest success had been in the presentation of its dance routines, not least in its brilliant chorus dancing, and it remained the yardstick by which Black musicals were judged for a decade or more.

15

Broadway in the Twenties

After *Shuffle Along* had proved conclusively that white audiences all over America responded enthusiastically to an all-Black show, there were several attempts to emulate its achievements, with varying degrees of success.

The greatest influence that the show had had was in the standard of dancing in musical comedies, revue and cabaret. Choreography became more elaborate, the execution more accomplished and more daring. The freedom of movement, too, was incomparably more open, more experimental – except in the case of the chorus lines which had greater precision, speed and vivacity. White dancers had been set new standards of performance by their Black counterparts, but although Blacks were frequently brought in to white shows, they always appeared in supporting roles, or to perform some solo turn, never as the stars.

The most successful of the shows which followed in the wake of *Shuffle Along* was, not surprisingly, *Runnin' Wild*, devised by two of the quartet who had staged *Shuffle Along*, Flournoy Miller and Aubrey Lyles. The great hit of the show was a male chorus number, danced to James P. Johnson's 'Charleston'. The dance had already established itself in dance halls and ballrooms, of course, but the way it was put over on stage by the chorus boys, The Dancing Redcaps, gave it a new lease of life. It was accompanied by exuberant hand-clapping and foot-stamping – just as it had always been performed in the south – and the effect of beating out complex rhythms in this way, never before seen on stage, had an electrifying effect on audiences.

Apart from the comedy team of Miller and Lyles, the featured dancers were Tommy Woods, who performed an acrobatic tap dance, and George Stamper who did another slow-motion dance which included the splits. There were two other excellent tap-dancers in the production, Lavinia Mack and Mae Barnes.

Running' Wild, produced by one of Broadway's most famous musical impresarios, George White, opened at the Colonial Theater on

62nd Street in October 1923, two years after *Shuffle Along*, but it had been preceded by several other shows featuring Black artists. Only three months after the opening of *Shuffle Along*, a show called *Put and Take* opened at the Town Hall, and it was the dancing of the chorus line that excited the critics and the audiences, one critic stating that it was better than any 'chorus of white girls on Broadway this season or for many seasons past'. The critic of the *Globe* remarked that after the 'slouch of many of our Broadway queens it is a relief to see . . . real snap and verve'.

Another Black show which impressed the critics with the precision and vitality of its chorus was *Strut Miss Lizzie*, which with *Plantation Revue* and *Liza* was one of three Negro productions to open on Broadway in 1922.

Plantation Revue developed from a vaudeville floor-show put together by the white owner-producer-director of the Plantation Club, Lew Leslie. The Plantation Club was a restaurant over the Winter Garden Theater, and soon after *Shuffle Along* had opened he persuaded its star, Florence Mills, to perform at his restaurant every night after the show. He wanted Mills to work for him full-time, and in order to get her he paid her three times the salary she was earning in *Shuffle Along* and he had to accept her dancer husband, Ulysses S. Thompson, as part of the deal. Thompson was an exceptionally fine dancer and his performances helped to make the Plantation Club a popular success.

A year later *Plantation Revue*, based on the best acts from the Plantation Club, opened at the Forty-Eighth Street Theater. Although the critics compared it unfavourably to *Shuffle Along* – it was, after all, only a revue, not a musical comedy – they noticed the virtuoso dancing of Thompson, calling him a 'jumping jack' and saying 'he throws himself around the stage in splendid fashion'. Thompson teamed with another dancer, Lou Keane, to do a Soft-shoe Shuffle to Stephen Foster's 1851 hit 'Swanee River', then both men performed their own specialities.

Liza opened at the Sixty-Third Street Theater when *Shuffle* moved out on tour and a few months later transferred to the Nora Bayes Theater on 44th Steet – the first all-Black show to play on Broadway during the regular season; all the others had been confined to the hot summer months. Two of the featured dancers in *Liza* were Rufus Greenlee and Thaddeus Drayton who performed the Virginia Essence in top hat and tails, wearing monocles and carrying canes. It was a new image for the Black dancer: gone were the overalls or the scarecrow clothes or even the flashy dressing of the city slicker; this was the elegance of Vernon and Irene Castle, the exemplars of smoothness and refinement, who, in their book of instructions for ballroom dancing,

► *Johnny Nit, one of the outstanding dancers who appeared in Harlem during the twenties.*

advised their pupils to avoid such 'ugly, ungraceful and unfashionable' styles as the Turkey Trot, the Bunny Hug and other Afro-Caribbean-based dances.

Another Black musical, *How Come*, opened at the Apollo Theater in April 1923, but only ran for a month or so. It was elaborately costumed but it seems that the cast tried too hard to be what they thought the audiences wanted; instead of a relaxed, infectious gaiety it was strident and brassy. Yet it included in the cast a brilliant Black performer, Johnny Nit, who was favoured with excellent reviews from the critics. His great speciality was the Buck and Wing which he performed at great speed and he was also a splendid tap-dancer.

The tap-dancing of the chorus girls was the most notable aspect of yet another all-Black show, *Chocolate Dandies*, in 1924 – despite having Josephine Baker as one of the leads. The chorus were drilled by a dancer called Charlie Davis, who taught them to tap complex rhythms in unison, a startling departure from the more usual high kicks and an effect that was to become almost a cliché in many revues and musicals

▲ *Florence Mills (left, standing on piano stool) in a scene from* Dixie to Broadway.

that followed. *Chocolate Dandies* opened at the Colonial Theater and ran for ninety-six performances.

A month later a mixed Black and white show, *Dixie to Broadway*, began a season at the Broadhurst Theater. (A version also ran in London, entitled *Dover to Dixie*.) It was another revue and included a number of excellent dancers amongst the cast. There were Florence Mills and her husband Ulysses S. Thompson who had scored such a hit in *Plantation Revue*, and also Johnny Nit who once more excelled with his furiously fast Buck and Wing. The white artists performed in the first half and the Black artists concluded the show, with a chorus line of eight girls, The Chocolate Drops, and eight boys, The Plantation Steppers.

It is interesting to note that *Chocolate Dandies* and *Dixie to Broadway* were running at the same time as Gershwin's *Lady Be Good*, starring Adele and Fred Astaire.

Performing on Broadway was, of course, prestigious for a Black dancer, but it brought poor financial reward. A dancer could earn much more in vaudeville and many Black artists preferred to stay with the vaudeville circuits, doing their speciality dances and becoming well known, if not famous, throughout the country. But around the middle of the twenties both Broadway and vaudeville were hit by a slump; Broadway regained its power of attraction towards the end of the decade but the decline of vaudeville was the beginning of the end for what had been a highly popular form of entertainment, its death-throes overshadowed by the coming of the 'talkies'.

In the three years between 1928 and 1930 Black revues and musicals made a big comeback on Broadway. Some were successful and some not but the most significant thing about them was that they had Black artists – dancers, singers and musicians – who either were, or became, real stars.

The singer Ethel Waters starred in *Africana*, singing such popular numbers as 'Dinah', 'Take your black bottom outside', and 'Shake that thing'. Waters may not have been credited as a dancer but she stopped the show with her shimmying and later wrote in her autobiography *His Eye is on the Sparrow*: 'I sure knew how to roll and quiver, and my hips would become whirling dervishes.' The dancers in the show included two artists billed as Baby and Bobby Goins doing something described as 'an athletic-aesthetic number', a pair called Taylor and Johnson who did a tap routine to the 'Black Bottom', and Snow Fisher and Pickaninny Hill, leading an ensemble, revived the Cake Walk.

In 1927 a show opened – and closed soon afterwards – called *Weather Clear – Track Fast*. It attracted little attention but it was notable in that it featured two Black dancers who were shortly to become one of the great dancing teams of the period. Billed as Joe Buck the Chicken Man and Jim Bubbles the Baltimore Sleeper, Buck and Bubbles had already achieved considerable fame in vaudeville and four years after *Weather Clear – Track Fast* they were to reach real stardom in the Ziegfeld *Follies* of 1931.

Another revue which was indifferently received by the critics, *Blackbirds* of 1928, was the vehicle in which the great Bill 'Bojangles' Robinson was 'discovered'. He included what was to be a signature piece, his Stair Dance, tapping up and down a flight of stairs, and his technique was so exciting and distinctive that the critics began to try to analyse just what he did with his feet that made his dancing so exceptional. They had no technical terms to help them – but they were able to explain that his taps were exceptionally clean, clear and sharply delineated in their rhythmic complexity. 'Bojangles', as he was universally known, not only had a consummate technique but, like Williams and Walker, possessed an innate showmanship and attractive stage

▶ *'Buck and Bubbles',
one of the notable
dancing teams of the
twenties and thirties
whose great success came
in the* Ziegfeld Follies *of
1931.*

personality that made his work stand out amongst his contemporaries.

In the same year as *Blackbirds* of 1928, *Keep Shufflin'* opened (its title obviously trying to cash in on the success of *Shuffle Along*); this show had moderate success, running for 104 performances. Although it mentioned no dancer by name the *New Yorker* remarked upon the 'tempestuous dancing for which the race is unsurpassed'.

1929 was a bonanza year for Black shows, five revues or musicals and one play being produced on Broadway. The most innovative was *Deep Harlem*, a play with singing and dancing which attempted to portray the history of the Afro-American race from Africa itself to Harlem. Critics and audiences expected the usual plantation-pickaninny-watermelon syndrome and were unresponsive to the show's attempt to be serious, calling it 'too self-conscious . . . too refined'. Only when the story reached Harlem and one or two stereotypes were discernible did they feel that the show succeeded as entertainment. One critic, however, recorded that 'two boys, named Cutout and Leonard, knew how to dance'.

The real names of Cutout and Leonard were Maceo Ellis and Leonard Reed who could both tap-dance but who specialised in eccentric dancing, a term which usually meant that the performer took a recognisable step or dance, say the Buck and Wing, the Turkey Trot or the Cake Walk, and performed it in his own way, perhaps speeding up or slowing down the tempo, adding acrobatics or doing it in comic costume with, maybe, enormous shoes or exceptionally baggy trousers.

The play *Harlem* which opened at the Apollo Theater included a party scene in which fifteen couples performed the Slow Drag in a manner which bewildered and even outraged some of the critics and audiences. The dance was performed with all the sensuality that would have been customary at a private party but would not have been seen in the ballroom, and this close-up of the authentic roots of Black dance perturbed a lot of people. Critics referred to the 'unholy violence', the 'steaming couples' who were 'writhing lustily through their barbaric dances'. The Shimmy and the Shake, the bumps and grinds, had suddenly been transformed from the relatively anodyne versions seen in revues and musicals into the unashamedly sexy stimulation of social dancing in the raw. The critic of the *Harlem News* prophesised that the police would stop the 'orgiastic exhibition'.

The police did not stop the show but ironically groups in Harlem felt that the Black image was being debased and the dancing was toned down.

Several other Black shows opened and closed on Broadway that season, some moderately successful. One, *Hot Chocolates*, established the name of 'Jazzlips' Richardson as an outstanding eccentric dancer. Another dancer, Roland Holder, achieved success doing an elegant Soft-shoe Shuffle in top hat and tails.

Of the several Black shows which opened in 1930, *Black Buddies* was the most important from the point of view of dancing. It was not particularly well received when it opened at the Liberty Theater, but it had been built around the personality of Bill 'Bojangles' Robinson and it ran for 113 performances. The plot and songs were considered poor but Robinson's dancing stopped the show, a big personal triumph for the dancer.

Robinson had a remarkable technique and one of his habits was to watch his own feet while performing, as if they had a life of their own; when he executed a series of steps he would grin at his feet and then at the audience as if they had all witnessed some form of magic. It was an effective trick, establishing a sort of conspiratorial rapport with the audience who were thus encouraged to concentrate their attention on his feet and his virtuosity.

But by 1930 the popularity of Black musicals and revues was waning. Perhaps there was too much similarity, too much repetition in the material. Many individual dancers besides Robinson were applauded for their abilities but the shows themselves seemed too inclined to feed off each other. The coming of the talkies and sound meant that film musicals could be produced with much more spectacle than was possible on stage. And then there was the Depression which affected every sort of Broadway show, when money from backers was hard to get and money from audiences was not forthcoming unless the critics were unanimous that the show was a hit.

In an attempt to merge an old and tried favourite with an approach to the reality of the social scene, *Shuffle Along* was revived in 1932 with a new plot based on the Depression; it lasted a week. Audiences did not want to be reminded of the harsh truths of the economy, they wanted escapism; and the new, luxurious picture palaces, where for a comparatively small sum they could be surrounded by sumptuous comfort and watch the stylish dancing of Fred Astaire and Ginger Rogers in *Flying Down to Rio*, provided it on a scale that revues and musicals simply could not match.

Perhaps the most significant aspect of all those Black-oriented shows on Broadway was not so much the acknowledgement that Black artists could attract an audience and sustain a show in the heart of America's theatre industry, but the development of jazz music and jazz dancers as an aesthetic synthesis. Many fine Black dancers emerged on Broadway during the twenties, but the advent of superb Black musicians and instrumentalists who accompanied them was of parallel importance. Amongst the Black musicians who played in Broadway shows and were later to become world famous on the jazz scene were Sidney Bechet, Clarence Williams, Joe Smith, Charlie Irvis, Leroy Smith, Louis Armstrong and Fats Waller. But it was in Harlem that the greatest association between jazz dancers and jazz musicians was to develop.

16

Harlem

During the first decade of the twentieth century there began what was to become a huge migration of Black citizens from the southern states of America to the north. It started as the result of years of crop failures together with the rise in the number of lynchings of Black people, then accelerated during the second decade because of World War I and the number of jobs available in the armaments industry. A census in 1916 recorded the migration from the south as some 350,000 people over a period of eighteen months.

At first the Black population of New York was on the west side, around 53rd Street; in 1913 blacks began to move uptown, north of Central Park to the area called Harlem. The move began because of a real-estate boom and a certain amount of over-development, with many of the apartment buildings under-tenanted. Black real-estate agents persuaded reluctant white property owners to rent their apartment houses to Black tenants. The growth of the Black population in Harlem was rapid, from 50,000 inhabitants in 1914 to 80,000 in 1920 to 200,000 ten years later.

▶ *Young hopefuls. An unidentified photograph of dancers taken in Harlem some time in the 1920s. Perhaps they were from a dancing school, perhaps they were auditioning for a show.*

The first all-Black theatre, the Crescent, opened in 1909. The Crescent held only about two hundred people, but in 1913, just a few doors away on 135th Street, the Lincoln Theater opened and could accommodate an audience of one thousand, and rapidly became the main venue for Black people.

The Lafayette Theater built in 1912 on Seventh Avenue between 131st and 132nd Streets at first segregated its audience and presented mainly white entertainers; the City Council issued a decree against this policy and the theatre was taken over by Black entertainers, the first Black orchestra playing there in 1913.

By the end of World War I Harlem was a well-established and thriving Black quarter with many clubs and theatres featuring the newly formed jazz groups, amongst which were the Apollo Theater on 125th Street, Small's Paradise on 135th Street, Leroy's also on 135th Street, the famous Cotton Club on Lenox Avenue and 142nd Street which catered for a whites-only audience, and the Savoy Ballroom also on Lennox Avenue between 140th and 141st Streets. In all these establishments dancers performed either in a professional or amateur capacity, frequently being billed as the main attraction. The Blacks from the south had brought with them their popular dance forms: The Black Bottom and the Charleston, Ballin' the Jack, the Shimmy, the Mooch and later the Lindy Hop, the Jitterbug, the Shag, the Suzy-Q, Truckin' and the Camel Walk: all of which found their way into the dance halls, into cabaret, revues, vaudeville, musical comedy, even 'serious' theatre.

Darktown Follies opened at the Lafayette Theater in 1913 and made it fashionable for whites to go uptown to Harlem to see the shows and take in the 'exotic' atmosphere of the Black quarter. Even when *Darktown Follies* moved downtown the whites still went to Harlem and went on going there for their entertainment for three decades.

Professional dancers often picked up dances that had been made popular in the dance halls and ballrooms, developed them and made them their speciality. The main ballroom of Harlem was the Savoy, which opened in March 1926. It was a large, grand establishment with a spacious lobby from which a marble staircase led up to the huge ballroom itself, stretching the length of a whole block with a double bandstand upon which two bands alternated. The establishment was maintained in first-class condition with a new floor installed every three years.

The original admission prices were thirty cents before 6 p.m., sixty cents before 8 p.m. and eighty-five cents after that. Keen dancers would try and afford at least one visit a week, but the popular night was, of course, Saturday, when the floor was so crowded there was no room for 'fancy stuff' and most people were content to 'shuffle along'. Tuesday was set aside for experts to practise their steps, but on Sundays it was the custom for celebrities to visit, many by special invitation, and there was an Opportunity Contest, with a first prize of ten dollars. Many aspirants to the ranks of professional dancers made their appearance in these contests. The north-east corner of the ballroom, known as 'Cats' Corner', was reserved for the professionals who would try out their new steps and routines, watched with great attention by everybody although it was an unwritten, carefully observed law that such steps were never copied.

Famous jazz and swing bands played at the Savoy, including those of Chick Webb (who introduced his new vocalist, Ella Fitzgerald), Fletcher Henderson, Duke Ellington and Cab Calloway. Competitions between the bands on the double bandstand were a great feature, and on one occasion, a contest between the bands of Chick Webb and Benny Goodman, 25,000 people were queuing round the block hoping to gain entrance.

The great dancing star of the Savoy was George 'Shorty' Snowden (he was five feet two inches) who for some years was the undisputed champion of the Cats' Corner and credited himself with the creation of the Lindy. (Other dancers, including Ray Bolger, made the same claim.)

Snowden achieved widespread renown when he won a marathon dance contest at the huge downtown New York ballroom, the Manhattan Casino. Fox Movietone News photographed Snowden's feet during the contest and when the interviewer asked him what step he was doing he replied: 'the Lindy'. What he was doing, in fact, was a 'breakaway' – a brief impromptu solo such as dancers had been inventing since the days of the Juba.

After his success at the Manhattan Casino, Snowden was given a lifetime's pass to the Savoy by its business manager, Charles Buchanan. On the crowded Saturday nights when he and similarly talented dancers would disdain to appear on the floor, he would be offered money to entertain the customers with his virtuoso dancing.

Other dancers who appeared at the Savoy and entertained the customers with their individual steps included Leon James (who danced the Lindy in the Marx Brothers' film *A Day at the Races*) and Albert Minns who later danced the Lindy as a full-time professional.

There were other popular ballrooms in Harlem – the New Star Casino, the Renaissance, the Alhambra – but the Savoy was the most important, the one where all the young dancers of the day, particularly those who aspired to being professional, went to practise and be seen.

The Lindy, or the Lindy Hop, is particularly associated with the

Savoy. It had one or two affinities with the Texas Tommy, inasmuch as it was essentially a dance for couples who at one point in the dance would break away and perform their own special steps before joining up again. The Lindy has a basic step, a syncopated two-step with the offbeat, or second beat, accented; this is repeated before the breakaway, depending very much on the music to which it is being performed. The synthesis between the music and the movement in the Lindy was an area of experiment where the instrumentalist and the dancer would inspire each other to more and more elaborate, wilder and wilder 'breaks'. The Lindy did much to develop 'swing' from the more traditional jazz rhythms. Whereas traditional jazz and the smaller groups which played it were suitable for a more up-and-down, jigging movement, the bigger bands which played at the Savoy essayed a more flowing style which resulted in dances of a smoother, 'swinging' rhythmic movement.

One of the instrumentalists who initiated a more frenetic manner in the Lindy was John 'Dizzy' Gillespie who played with Teddy Hill's band at the Savoy. His 'crazy licks' would set the dancers inventing equally crazy stuff, a kind of challenge match which, although it was improvisatory, created a number of steps which remained as favourites in the Lindy breakaways.

The audience – particularly the whites from down town who went to see the 'black cats' performing – were also a challenge to the Lindy dancers to devise and practise ever more complicated steps. This led to the introduction of acrobatics and the evolution of two distinct schools: the dancers who specialised in floor steps, and those who used air steps or rather, movements. The 'old guard', Shorty Snowden, Leon James and Leroy Jones, disapproved of such innovations as the air steps; it was a younger group, which included Albert Minns, who resorted to acrobatics, many of their movements based on judo throws.

For some years the Lindy – later much more widely known as the Jitterbug, a word which in jazz parlance had sexual connotations – remained the preserve of a small number of dance enthusiasts before it suddenly seemed to appear out of nowhere as a popular craze fomented by the brilliance of Benny Goodman's swing band. Goodman's performances at the Paramount Theater in New York set his young listeners 'jitterbugging in the aisles', to such an extent that the fire department was called in to check the safety of the balconies. This was publicised from coast to coast and the excitement it generated created a dance craze that had its origins amongst the stylish exponents of Harlem. In ballrooms and nightclubs, vaudeville and the cinema, the more staid members of the public saw young people hurling each other

Left: The famous Savoy ballroom, on Lenox Avenue, Harlem. Opposite: Inside the Savoy, dancers performing the Lindy. These pictures were taken in the 1940s, the height of the 'jitter bugging' era.

about with wild abandon, yet no matter how acrobatic or dangerous the movement the dancers were able to maintain the beat and the swinging rhythm of the music. If the Charleston had ousted the waltz, if the Black Bottom usurped the foxtrot, the Lindy/Jitterbug swept all before it during the thirties and much of the forties, a dance style with its roots in Afro-Caribbean movement, evolved over a century.

It was not long before several professional Lindy dance teams were formed, most of them under the management of Herbert White, the legendary semi-criminal bouncer at the Savoy. He employed about seventy-two dancers, including the most famous teams, the Savoy Hoppers and Whitey's Lindy Hoppers, who toured the country appearing in nightclubs, vaudeville, Broadway musicals and films. White treated them like slaves, giving them small wages and cheating them out of contract fees: when the contract stipulated travel by train he would send them by bus and pocket the difference. White died a comparatively rich man; the Savoy Ballroom was pulled down in 1959 to make way for a housing development.

The Lafayette Theater, which at first operated a segregated policy, later presented a number of Black dancers who specialised in various forms: eccentric dancing, character, tap and vaudeville turns. *Darktown Follies* opened there in 1913 and the playhouse later developed its own stock repertory company which presented versions of Broadway hits and melodramas, but dance and dancers continued to appear there for many years, as they did at the Apollo Theater, the Cotton Club, Leroy's and Small's Paradise.

Bill 'Bojangles' Robinson was perhaps the most famous, but amongst a number of outstanding dancers were Brady Jackson – Jigsaw Jackson the Human Corkscrew – who appeared at the Cotton Club with Duke Ellington and his band, an eccentric dancer whose speciality was to lie with his jaw on the floor while his feet tapped out a rhythm; Henry 'Rubberlegs' Williams, another eccentric whose version of Truckin' was also a success at the Cotton Club; and Earl 'Snake Hips' Tucker, who performed at the Lafayette Theater and was also a regular at the Cotton Club and Connie's Inn.

Tucker specialised – as his self-styled soubriquet indicates – in a form of dance movement in which he rotated his pelvis in a sinuously suggestive manner. He also performed the Belly Roll, a series of wavy motions from chest to pelvis; his whole torso seemed boneless and during the performance he would fix the audience with a baleful glare like a snake hypnotising a rodent. Tucker had an off-stage reputation of being a mean man – mean in the American sense of hard and vicious; he carried a razor and had a violent temper.

► *'Snake Hips' Earl Tucker, one of the specialist dancers who appeared in Harlem's heyday and who, together with Bill 'Bojangles' Robinson, was one of the most volatile characters of the era.*

For all the fame of the Lafayette, the Apollo, the Savoy, the Cotton Club, Leroy's and Small's Paradise, perhaps the most interesting – and least known – centre of dance in Harlem was the Hoofers' Club. Just past the stage door of the Lafayette Theater on Seventh Avenue was a gambling establishment, the Comedy Club, where it was possible to play poker or pool at any time day or night. In a back room, bare but for an old upright piano and benches round the walls, it was possible for dancers to practise their routines as long as they wanted without payment; except perhaps for buying the piano-player the odd drink. But as the pianist was more often than not the proprietor, Lonnie Hicks, who liked dancers and did not want to make money from them, even that was unusual.

The smoky back room was the rendezvous for all serious dancers, whether they were the successful ones, like 'Bojangles' and 'Snake Hips' or tyros wishing to emulate their achievements. The front rooms, too, were filled with dancers: 'Bojangles' played pool there and reputedly used to lay his goldplated gun on the table when playing a difficult shot. Like 'Snake Hips' he had the reputation of possessing a volatile temperament. But it was the back room where the serious business took place and many a routine that brought success in vaudeville, cabaret or musical comedy originated in that raunchy environment.

There is no doubt that for more than two decades, from the twenties to the forties, Harlem was the centre of Black dance in America. Only a few dancers made it to the top and their success was, in many if not most cases, comparatively shortlived: a number of notable dancers ended up doing menial tasks in factories or as janitors or doormen. But, lacking the organisation and infrastructure that exists for dancers today with schools and studios and teachers, it was a period of excitement, energy and experiment, providing a climate where the embryo dancer could achieve his ambition of becoming a star.

17

Tap, Techniques and Teachers

Tap-dancing, like jazz, seemed to have had no definite beginning. It evolved from other forms, some immediately discernible, others more obscure, until it burgeoned suddenly, as jazz did, like an organic growth that appeared to have its roots in a dozen places.

The most immediate precursors of tap would seem to be the Irish jig and the Lancashire clog dance – even an amalgam of both, which Black slaves frequently emulated when they saw them being performed by white folks down south. But the Black performer had his own tap techniques, a way of producing percussive rhythms with the feet, along with clapping of the hands and slapping of the torso, in those days when drums were forbidden.

It was the Buck and Wing, evolving from the popular clog dances of the late nineteenth century and using a variety of steps, that was important as a formative influence on tap-dancing, particularly with the advent of ragtime around the turn of the century and the development of jazz with its elaborately syncopated rhythms. The Soft-shoe Shuffle (soft, leather-soled shoes, as opposed to wooden-soled shoes for clog-dancing) demanded elegance in its presentation, and the Virginia Essence, where the feet rolled rapidly in a heel-and-toe progression to produce the effect of gliding over the floor, was the epitome of such dances. By contrast the Buck and Wing needed accentuated rhythm for its effects, and taps or tapping, which were the basis of so many Black dance forms, were an ideal way of accenting the rhythms.

In their definitive book on American vernacular dance, *Jazz Dance*, Marshall and Jean Stearns refer to a dancer, Laurence 'Baby' Jackson, as crediting four dancers with the evolution of tap: 'King' Rastus Brown, an expert Buck and Wing dancer who frequently added taps to accent his performances; Bill 'Bojangles' Robinson who danced on his toes and perfected all manner of rhythmic complexities; Eddie Rector who provided body motion and elegance; and John W. Bubbles who added even greater complexity to tap steps.

There is no doubt that these four creative dancers did much to evolve the technique of tap but it would be claiming too much to say they originated it.

Brown, a little-known dancer outside his own narrow sphere, but held in great esteem by those who saw him, seems to have emerged in New York around 1903, although reports differ as to where he came from originally. He was reputed to have won a Buck-dancing contest at Madison Square Garden in 1910 and he was a frequent and highly respected visitor to the Hoofers' Club in Harlem, where his demonstrated routines were watched with admiration by both his peers and the younger generation anxious to learn. His repertoire was extensive: 'he could imitate anything', one observer remarked, including the Cake Walk, the Irish jig, the Sand Dance (a soft-shoe variation performed on sand that had been sprinkled on the stage to give a distinctive swishing sound to the steps) and various national dances.

Yet around the same time that Brown was impressing the cognoscenti with his shuffles and tap, Alice Whitman, the youngest of the Whitman Sisters, was being billed as 'The Queen of Taps', which would indicate that the style was fairly widely developed early in the century.

During the twenties and thirties there were many splendid tap dancers, both Black and white, from John W. Bubbles to Fred Astaire.

Bubbles, who real name was John Sublett, began his theatrical career as a singer but he wanted to dance as well. His early attempts at the Hoofers' Club were mocked by some of the professionals there, so, while touring California as a singer on the vaudeville circuit he practised tap-dancing assiduously; on his return to New York his success as a dancer was immediate. At the age of ten Bubbles had teamed with a six-year-old, Ford Lee 'Buck' Washington, and as Buck and Bubbles they maintained their act together – Buck the musician and Bubbles the dancer – for over twenty years. Buck emulated Bubbles' fast, syncopated tap-dancing in a lazy, nonchalant manner in between his piano-playing; Bubbles' subsequent solo would be performed at an even greater tempo. He was famous for the speed with which he performed his dances, for the many variations he could build from one sequence, and for the stamina with which he could maintain his extemporary routines.

In 1935 Bubbles was chosen by George Gershwin to play the role of Sportin' Life in his opera *Porgy and Bess*; in 1943 he appeared in MGM's all-Black musical *Cabin in the Sky*, which featured Lena Horne, Ethel Waters, Cab Calloway and Louis Armstrong; and in 1948 he starred in Goldwyn's *A Song is Born* with Danny Kaye and Virginia Mayo. During the sixties Bubbles made frequent appearances on American television shows; he died in 1967.

Bubbles was a regular visitor to the Hoofers' Club but he rarely condescended to tutor the young tyros there although many benefited from watching his workouts. He did have one young protégé in whom he took an interest however: Charles 'Honi' Coles.

Coles spanned some thirty years of tap dance, from its heyday in the thirties until its general demise in the sixties. He grew up in the twenties in Philadelphia, a city where tap-dancing was particularly popular, from the vaudeville theatres to every back alley and street corner where amateurs practised and danced for pennies. Coles practised basic steps at home until he had perfected an extensive routine. In 1931 he joined a group called The Three Millers and opened at the Lafayette Theater in Harlem where they danced on narrow planks five feet above the stage. But it was the height of the Depression and after that engagement no more work was forthcoming so Coles returned to Philadelphia.

During the enforced break Coles practised incessantly, trying new steps and new ideas. He speeded things up and he extended the duration of his steps, putting together longer, sixteen-bar units where most tap-dancers of the time chopped up tunes into eight-bar breaks. When he returned to New York in 1932 he had no difficulty in finding work and it was at this time that he became acquainted with Bubbles at the Hoofers' Club. He had a solo spot with Cab Calloway's band and while travelling with this ensemble he met and teamed up with Charles 'Cholly' Atkins.

Both Coles and Atkins joined the army in 1943; after the war they formed a team, starring at the Apollo Theater in Harlem for several seasons. Apart from their elegant tap routines – both dancers were insistent that they combine their tap with stylish body movements – they developed a particularly effective Soft-shoe Shuffle, danced at an extremely slow tempo, a performance that was described as 'lyrical' and which was in dramatic contrast to their fast, percussive tapping.

Coles and Atkins danced with most of the famous big swing bands of the time, with Cab Calloway, Louis Armstrong, Charlie Barnet, Lionel Hampton, Billie Eckstine and Count Basie. In 1948 they toured Britain with great success. In 1949 they joined the cast of the musical *Gentlemen Prefer Blondes*, their routine erroneously credited to ballet choreographer Agnes de Mille, and stayed with the show for two years. They played in many revivals of musicals, such as *Kiss Me Kate*, and then, as tap began to be replaced more and more by ballet and modern dance, they broke up. In 1955 they went to work together again in Las Vegas, then worked with Pearl Bailey for eighteen months before finding themselves out of work once more. Atkins turned to coaching young dancers and Coles became production manager at the Apollo Theater.

▶ *'Honi' Coles and 'Cholly' Atkins at the Apollo Theater, Harlem, in the 1940s. One of the great 'class' acts, Coles and Atkins' partnership lasted more than thirty years.*

Throughout the sixties Coles and Atkins gave several special performances at such events as the Newport Jazz Festival and made many appearances on television shows in America, where they demonstrated most of the classic tap steps, the Buck and Wing, the Time Step and various pioneering styles, including their own inimitable Soft-shoe Shuffle. At the beginning of the eighties the author was privileged to see 'Honi' Coles demonstrate early tap routines, the Sand Dance and the Soft-shoe Shuffle at the Riverside Studios in London. Coles and Atkins were the ultimate example of what other protagonists of American vernacular dance call 'a class act', and there can be no higher praise than that.

A class act referred to dances done with elegance and style, the executants more often than not in dinner jackets or top hat and tails. In the thirties and forties this was differentiated from the 'flash acts', a term which referred to a combination of steps and acrobatics; such a performance could even include Russian folk steps such as the Kazotsky, Spanish flamenco, and ballet, interspersed with tap.

As early as 1900 and during the great popularity of the minstrels, Black dancers had begun to mix acrobatics and tumbling with their Cake Walks, the result of vaudeville shows where the dancers were in constant contact with circus artists. Somersaults, back-flips and cartwheels began to be used in all sorts of dance routines and repertoires, and this tendency gathered force during the development of tap as rivalries increased and the need to 'top' each other's performance became more and more insistent.

There were literally dozens of 'flash acts', some solo but the majority made up of teams where, after a synchronised entrance number, each member of the troupe would perform his speciality solo leading to the finale, once again performed in unison. In this way the act could be spun out to ten or fifteen minutes; such dancing was exhausting – and often dangerous – and the solo performer could not expect to sustain it longer than a few minutes. Some acts incorporated singing, although the performers were usually too breathless for this, and many included clowning with their tumbling, or some form of grotesque characterisation such as elderly people suddenly leaping into an animated dance or acrobatics – a throwback to the popular Eph and Dinah sketch of the medicine shows and carnivals.

One of the first notable 'flash acts' was performed by The Crackerjacks who evolved from a group known as The Watermelon Trust. This last troupe consisted of a comedian called Grundy, an acrobatic dancer, Sherman Coates, and their two wives. When Grundy and Coates broke up in 1914, Coates' wife Lulu organised a troupe called Lulu Coates and Her Crackerjacks, which included three young dancers who were also aspiring acrobats. When Mrs Coates retired in 1922, two of those dancers, Archie Ware and Harry Irons, joined two others, Clifford Carter and Raymond Thomas, as The Crackerjacks, organised with Mrs Coates' blessing.

The formation of The Crackerjacks varied over the years from four to six members, drawn from a total of twelve, only four of whom were not acrobats. They appeared in many big shows at the Cotton Club and on Broadway, and they toured America from coast to coast. Their act included comedy routines, singing and tap-dancing mixed with acrobatics and tumbling, and most of it was performed to swinging rhythms. The Crackerjacks set the pace and style for other similar troupes and lasted thirty years, finally breaking up in 1952.

The fierceness of the competition led the 'flash acts' to attempt more and more dangerous movements, some from gymnastics, some from ballet, and many of the participants had not had proper training; they rarely even practised the generally accepted principle of warming-up before going into hair-raising stunts, or attempting steps and movements that only properly trained dancers and acrobats should perform. The result was that a number of dancers suffered serious injuries, torn muscles and ligaments, and broken and fractured bones, which in many cases resulted in being crippled for life.

One step that was frequently used in 'flash-dancing' was the colloquially termed 'splits' or, to give the step its balletic name, *grand écart*. It was frequently used as the culmination of a dance, the climax of a movement, because of its spectacular effect and its use as a punctuation mark in conjunction with the conclusion of a drum break. In nearly all cases, however, the 'splits' were faked, with the dancer bending the rear leg, or resting on the calf muscle; few of them had the necessary balletic training with its emphasis on turn out from the hips which is essential if the step is to be properly performed. Nevertheless, crashing down on the floor with the legs seemingly splayed apart was a satisfying conclusion to many 'flash acts' and deceived most uninitiated audiences.

One acrobatic tap ensemble, The Three Little Words, composed of Joe Jones, Charles Blackstone and Billy Yates, began their act with a gentle Soft-shoe Shuffle, progressed to a three-part challenge dance and ended with Jones running up the wall and doing a back-flip into the splits, then jumping to his feet again. The Three Little Words did much to popularise the Harlem club run by the jazz trombonist Dickie Wells on Seventh Avenue, during the Depression. The group remained together from 1927 until 1942.

The two most spectacular 'flash acts' were two sets of brothers: The Berry Brothers and The Nicholas Brothers, great rival acts which, on one memorable occasion, appeared on the same bill together in direct competition.

There were three Berry brothers: Ananias and Jimmy who were born in New Orleans, and Warren who was born in Denver. The family made its way to the West Coast; the older brothers entered an amateur contest in Hollywood in 1929 and Jimmy got a job in *Our Gang* two-reel comedies. In 1929 Ananias and Jimmy appeared as a duo with Duke Ellington at the Cotton Club in Harlem, where they appeared on and off for four years. In 1932 they appeared at the opening of Radio City Music Hall. When Ananias married, Warren took over his routines; then, after a couple of years, Ananias returned and for the next decade

▶ *The three Berry Brothers: Ananias (left), Warren (centre), James (right). Perhaps the greatest of the so-called 'flash' acts, the Berry Brothers were strong rivals of the Nicholas Brothers.*

▶ *The three Berry Brothers: Ananias (left), Warren (centre), James (right). Perhaps the greatest of the so-called 'flash' acts, the Berry Brothers were strong rivals of the Nicholas Brothers.*

the three brothers danced together with tremendous success. Everything they did was carefully syncopated – one part of their act included much play with canes – and they included high kicks and strutting, tap-dancing and acrobatics. The choreographer Nick Castle, who worked with The Berry Brothers in Hollywood on the film *You're My Everything*, credited them (if that is the term) with the introduction of the 'splits' into such dancing.

The Nicholas Brothers, Fayard and Harold, grew up in Philadelphia, sharing the same ambience as 'Honi' Coles. Their parents came from New Orleans, their father a drummer and their mother a pianist in their own pit band at the Standard Theatre in Philadelphia, where the four-year-old Fayard watched all the dancers and acrobats of the day, including Alice Whitman and Bill 'Bojangles' Robinson. Both brothers began practising their own routines on street corners before they had reached their teens, and were hired for a local radio programme and also appeared

▶ *The two Nicholas Brothers: Harold (left) and Fayard in the film* Big Broadcast of 1935. *They began their career at an early age and grew to be the most celebrated of the 'class' acts.*

at the local theatres. When they were at the Pearl Theater they were seen by a New York producer who hired them for the Lafayette Theater in Harlem. After that they went to the Cotton Club, where they stayed for two years. When they opened there in 1932, Fayard was fourteen and Harold was eight, both of them dressed in top hats and tails, their precocious sophistication a great hit with the audiences. Their routine included tap-dancing and acrobatics, all performed with an air of elegant insouciance, rather like miniature Astaires.

Their career developed rapidly: from the Cotton Club they went to Hollywood where they appeared in the 1935 film *Kid Millions,* starring Eddie Cantor and Ann Sothern. There were more appearances at the Cotton Club, another film *The Big Broadcast of 1935,* then the Ziegfeld *Follies* on Broadway, a tour of Britain with *Blackbirds,* Radio City Music Hall, and another Broadway musical *Babes in Arms,* choreographed by no less a person than George Balanchine from whom they learned much.

The great confrontation with The Berry Brothers came in 1938 at the Cotton Club, which in 1936 had moved from Harlem to mid-town New York on Broadway and 48th Street. The Berry Brothers had been placed last on the bill by the producer, Herman Stark, who also happened to be The Nicholas Brothers' manager. It was a deliberate challenge: The Berry Brothers had to 'top' their rivals or die a theatrical death. Ananias had a plan. At the conclusion of their act Ananias and Jimmy sprinted up the stairs behind the band, took a flying leap over the heads of the musicians and landed, twelve feet below, in the splits, coinciding with Warren who had just come out of a back somersault into the splits himself. All three brothers managed to finish on the last note of the music: it was the apotheosis of the 'flash act'.

In 1951 Ananias, who had suffered a number of injuries, died at the age of thirty-nine and the act broke up. By contrast, The Nicholas Brothers went from strength to strength: in 1941 they appeared with The Inkspots in the film *The Great American Broadcast*; that same year they made what was their most telling film appearance, dancing on and off the platform of a railroad car in the famous 'Chattanooga Choo-Choo' number in the film *Sun Valley Serenade*, starring the ice skater Sonja Henie and Glenn Miller and his orchestra.

Fayard and Harold Nicholas played all over the world, appearing in cabaret, in musicals, in films and on television; even being featured in Bob Hope's Christmas show for the troops in Vietnam in 1965. There have been many arguments about the relative merits of The Berry Brothers and The Nicholas Brothers, but it would seem that The Nicholas Brothers were the best, most elegant tap ensemble, while The Berry Brothers were the ultimate 'flash act'.

During the twenties and thirties, the time of the Whitman Sisters, Bill 'Bojangles' Robinson, John Bubbles, Charles 'Cholly' Atkins and Charles 'Honi' Coles, there were very few teachers to whom such artists could go for formal instruction – even if they could have afforded it. Most of those dancers, and their lesser contemporaries, were self-taught, watching older professionals practise their routines backstage or at the Hoofers' Club, entering amateur contests, dancing for pennies on street corners, working on routines from the knowledge of one or two basic steps repeated over and over. Sometimes – very occasionally – someone like 'King' Rastus Brown or Bill Robinson would show an interest in another dancer and demonstrate an eight-bar sequence or some special step, or the dancer would have the benefit of working under a celebrated choreographer, but mostly it was a matter of thinking up ideas of their own then incorporating them into the Cake Walk, the Buck and Wing, the Charleston or some other well-established step or style.

Certain dancers who had gained success on the stage in cabaret, vaudeville or musical comedy found a lucrative sideline in teaching wealthy members of society how to do the latest ballroom steps; even Black servants – maids, valets, footmen and chauffeurs – were given extra duties tutoring masters and mistresses in the fine art of the Black Bottom or the Big Apple.

For the professionals, Hollywood provided another source of income, teaching the stars how to do the popular ballroom dances or working on routines for musicals. For example, Bill 'Bojangles' Robinson coached Shirley Temple for her role in *The Little Colonel* in 1935.

One dancer who was particularly sought after by the studios was Willie Covan. He had been the star performer in a family quartet, Willie and his wife and his brother Dewey and his wife, known as The Four Covans. Willie went to Hollywood where he was recommended to MGM by Eleanor Powell and, during a career spanning two or three decades, gave personal coaching to such stars as Mae West, Jeanette McDonald, Shirley Temple (aged eleven), Marilyn Maxwell, Robert Taylor, Mickey Rooney, Kirk Douglas, Gregory Peck, Mary Tyler Moore and Dick Van Dyke. Significantly Covan never received any screen credit for his work.

Perhaps the best known Black coach-cum-choreographer was Clarence 'Buddy' Bradley. Born in Harrisburg, Pennsylvania, he was still very young when his father died and he was brought up, very strictly, by his mother. She died when he was fourteen and he went to live with a brother-in-law in Utica, New York, where he was put to work in a hotel. After a few weeks he ran away to New York City where he found work as an elevator boy and stayed in a lodging house full of show people, including many dancers.

Like so many of his contemporaries he learned the basic steps of American vernacular dance, including tap, on the sidewalks of Harlem but felt too amateur to venture into the Hoofers' Club. Quite by chance he was offered a job as a chorus boy at Connie's Inn, a big nightclub next to the Lafayette Theater. He worked diligently, watching the routines of all the visting stars, until he was considered one of the best young dancers in Harlem. Because of his expertise and charming manner he was offered a job teaching in a small downtown studio that had opened on West 46th Street. One of his first 'pupils' was the singer and dancer Irene Delroy who was then starring in the *Greenwich Village Follies of 1928*. Realising that Delroy could not manage the complicated wings and tap steps that he put together he created a dance routine for her that was tailored to her limited technique; it was such a success that the director of the show asked Bradley to re-choreograph the entire production. From that moment he was in continual demand, especially because of his flair for creating dances that were based on the talents of the individual artist.

Bradley coached the stars in several of Florenz Ziegfeld's *Follies* and George White's *Scandals*, including creating a solo for Fred Astaire's sister, Adele Astaire. Like Covan, Bradley never received any official recognition for the wonderfully creative work he did on American shows, despite creating routines for such stars as Lucille Ball, Clifton Webb and Eleanor Powell.

In 1933 Bradley was invited by the British musical impresario Charles Cochrane to choreograph the London production of *Evergreen*. It was an unprecedented responsibility for a Black artist; he was in charge of sixty-four dancers: sixteen regular dancers, sixteen Tiller girls, sixteen chorus girls and sixteen chorus boys. It was the first time a Black man had choreographed an entire white show and he received full credit for it on the programme.

Bradley stayed on in London, an important creative force in popular dance. He worked on several Cochrane musicals, created a cabaret act for Vera Zorina and Anton Dolin, coached Jessie Matthews in many of her films and worked in France, Italy, Spain and Switzerland. Bradley's was an enormous talent based on wide experience and the inborn ability to teach. It is a pity that his talent did not receive the recognition it deserved in his own country where his reputation should stand alongside such choreographers as Busby Berkeley, Nick Charles, Robert Fosse, Michael Kidd and Gower Champion, but Europe's gain was certainly America's loss.

18

Josephine Baker

Like Clarence 'Buddy' Bradley, Josephine Baker achieved her greatest successes as an expatriate: whereas Bradley found fame and fortune in London, Baker spent most of her career as a celebrity in Paris.

Baker was born in St Louis, Missouri, in 1906, one of four children in a very poor family. One of her earliest memories was the violent, murderous destruction of the shanty town in which they lived by a white lynch mob; the experience left an indelible impression on the young child who resolved to escape from the squalor of such an environment.

Baker was born illegitimate, her mother Black, her father Spanish, a man who quite quickly disappeared from the scene to be replaced with a Black surrogate father. Baker left school at the age of eight to help supplement the family income, taking such varied work as a maid, a babysitter and kitchen help.

As an adolescent Baker watched the dancers in a local vaudeville theatre and did some part-time chorus work there herself. At fifteen she joined a travelling troupe which included the blues singer Bessie Smith. When the show closed Baker spent what few dollars she had on the train fare to New York, where she auditioned for *Shuffle Along*. She was considered too young for the chorus but was taken on as a dresser. With an opportunism that manifested itself throughout her career, she proposed that she should take over the role of one of the chorus girls who had become pregnant and she was given the part. Whether or not she simply could not dance the routines, or whether she clowned around on the end of the chorus line as a means of drawing attention to herself, is uncertain; whatever the reason she was noticed by the audience who responded enthusiastically to her antics, and the management paid her the astronomical fee of 125 dollars a week to continue her chorus-line clowning. It was not all comic tricks, however; the critic of the *New York Post* wrote that 'there was something about her rhythm, her smile and her impudent grace that made her stand out.' The columnist Walter Winchell later put it more succinctly: 'Josephine Baker has it all – class, talent – and ding dong.'

After *Shuffle Along* Baker appeared in *Chocolate Dandies*, produced by two of the quartet responsible for *Shuffle Along*, Eubie Blake and Noble Sissle, who considered Baker their protégée. The show ran at the Colonial Theater for nearly a hundred performances; when it closed Baker appeared in the floor show at Lew Leslie's Plantation Club. While performing there she was invited to star in *La Revue Nègre*, an American production which opened at the Champs Elysée Theatre in Paris in October 1925. Baker was an immediate, sensational success, the toast of Paris, the epitome of the latest craze, *le jazz hot*. She was just nineteen.

In America Baker's light skin colour had been something of an impediment, not light enough to pass as white, too light to seem Black enough for an all-Black show: one of her childhood nicknames was 'Pinky' and in her first appearance in vaudeville she had had to black-up her face. But for Parisians it was dark enough to seem exotic, and her vivacity, her rhythmic sense, her volatile stage presence combined in a sensuous, exciting mixture in a city where there was no colour problem.

Baker soon learned to play off one management against another. While appearing in *La Revue Nègre* she left the show to join the *Folies Bergère* for more money and star billing, and was promptly sued for breach of contract. She returned to *La Revue Nègre*, which was then in Berlin, and was so captivated by that city (then in its wildest phase under the Weimar Republic) that she refused to return to Paris and the *Folies Bergère*. She was also offered work with the great German producer Max Reinhardt. Finally she was lured back by the promise of even more money and star billing. Her appearance caused another sensation, naked except for a girdle of rubber bananas.

It was the beginning of a long association with the *Folies Bergère* throughout the twenties and thirties. She was admired, feted, celebrated in a way she never would have been in her homeland. Even more important she could command the sort of salary that only the top white stars could get in America. Her theatrical costumes were designed by one of the world's greatest designers, Erté; she drove a Délage with snakeskin upholstery; she appeared everywhere with her pet leopard, Chiquita; her name was romantically linked with the most famous people in the world, from Mussolini to members of European aristocracy.

Baker repeated her Parisian success throughout Europe, from London to Madrid, Vienna to Budapest. She had an equally great success in South America, but her return to New York, opening in Ziegfeld's *Follies* on Christmas Eve 1935, was less than successful. One or two critics made polite mention of her, others were openly critical;

▶ *Josephine Baker in her celebrated costume of a girdle of bananas with which she astonished and delighted Paris in 1925.*

Fanny Bryce got the rave reviews. Baker's subsequent cabaret performances at the Mirage on East 54th Street were more successful, the critics considering her talents more suited to the intimacy of cabaret than the open spaces of a big theatre. Baker returned to Paris and the usual adulation she received there.

In 1937 she married a French businessman, Jean Lion. Early the following year she lost her baby through a miscarriage; she divorced Lion in 1939.

During World War II Baker took refuge in North Africa where, despite a long illness, she worked with the Free French forces in support of General de Gaulle, reputedly in liaison with undercover agents and later entertained Allied troops in North Africa and in Europe after the Allied invasion. In 1947 she married a French bandleader, Jo Bouillon, who also managed her business affairs.

In 1950, while in Havana in Cuba, Baker received an offer to appear at the elegant Copa City Club in Miami. She agreed to perform on condition that the club was open to both Blacks and whites – an almost impossible condition in a city where, at that time, segregation was strictly enforced. Baker remained adamant and it was finally agreed that the club would be open to everyone. Baker's appearance was a triumphant success – but it was accounted an even greater triumph for the Civil Rights movement.

In 1951 Harlem, New York, proclaimed a Josephine Baker day. She was received like royalty, thousands of people turning out in the streets to welcome her. Speeches were made in honour of her achievements in defence of the Civil Rights laws, there were brass bands, cocktail parties, a ball attended by the French Ambassador, Gypsy Rose Lee, Frederic March and the Nobel Peace Prize winner Dr Ralph Bunche. But Baker's reception aroused segregationist feeling against her. In Atlanta she cancelled her appearance after being turned away from three hotels. There was a scene at the Stork Club where the management did their best not to serve her. Walter Winchell, the columnist, who had admired her performance in Miami, accused her of being a Communist. Her theatrical triumphs were soured by the hostility she aroused because of her support for the Civil Rights movement.

Throughout the rest of the fifties and sixties Baker continued to appear in cabaret around the world, although her successes were more modest and more limited than in the thirties. She devoted much time and her dwindling financial resources to establishing a home for her twelve adopted children at Les Milandes, a chateau in the Dordogne. Faced with bankruptcy, she was forced to abandon Les Milandes in 1968. At the same time she separated from Bouillon.

Josephine Baker in a typical Folies Bergère *costume. Many of her gowns were created by the great designer Erté.*

With her twelve children and numerous pets (throughout her life Baker had had a menagerie that travelled with her) she took a tiny apartment in Paris where she was offered the chance to appear at a small nightclub, La Goulue, owned by the actor Jean-Claude Brialy who, during Baker's last years, did much to support her. Her appearance there was a great success and led to an invitation to appear at a charity gala at the Sporting Club in Monte Carlo. This, too, was a great personal triumph which in turn produced further offers to appear in cabaret around the world as well as an appearance at the London Palladium.

Princess Grace of Monaco was instrumental in finding a permanent home for Baker and her children at Roquebrune, just outside Monte Carlo. In 1975 she opened in a revue entitled simply *Josephine* at the small Bobino Theatre in Paris; during the run she celebrated fifty years on the Paris stage. She died just over a week later on April 12, 1975.

On November 7, 1976, the Variety Club Foundation of New York presented a special gala tribute to Josephine Baker at the Metropolitan Opera House, Lincoln Center, in aid of orphan children. Amongst the glittering and fashionable audience was the nonagenarian Eubie Blake, one of the original producers of *Shuffle Along*.

19

Asadata Dafora and Concert Dance

At the very turn of the century in 1900 and 1902 Bert Williams and George Walker produced and appeared in two shows, *A Senegambian Carnival* and *In Dahomey*, in which they attempted to present West African tribal dances in a serious manner, that is in the way such dances would be performed in their Senegalese or Dahomean villages. They were not a success; the image of the Black American was already too fixed, too stereotyped, for audiences to see the link with such alien figures. It is ironic that Williams and Walker were largely responsible for the popularity of the 'plantation' Negro and the accretion of comic characteristics that he had acquired. Dahomeans were no substitute for the genial Uncle Tom or the strutting Cake-Walker.

As a result *In Dahomey* had to be changed from its original conception before it achieved popularity. In London it ran for seven months in 1903 and, most ironic of all, it made the Cake Walk an international craze. It was to be three decades before audiences would see Afro-Americans in serious concert dance as opposed to the popular forms of dance in cabaret, vaudeville and musical comedy.

A year before George Walker retired, in 1907, Hemsley Winfield was born in Yonkers, New York. His mother, Jeroline was a playwright and in 1927 he organised a group of dancers to appear in a play she had written, *Wade in the Water*, at the Cherry Lane Theater in Greenwich Village. Although he had no formal training as a dancer himself, he later filled in for the actress playing the title role in his company's production of Oscar Wilde's *Salome*, performing the Dance of the Seven Veils. The success he achieved in this rather extraordinary circumstance encouraged him to take up dance as his profession and at the age of twenty-five he formed the Negro Art Theater in Harlem, which later became the Negro Art Theatre Dance Group. Somewhat ambitiously, the group consisted of eighteen dancers (many of today's dance groups are not so large) and they were sometimes known as the New Negro Art Dancers.

The first performance given by Winfield's company was on April 29, 1931 in a tiny theatre on top of the Chanin Building on Lexington Avenue at 42nd Street in New York – The Theater in the Clouds.

The programme included two solos by Edna Guy entitled Figure from Angkor-Vat and Temple Offering. There seems some confusion about whether the solos were actually choreographed by Ruth St Denis or by Edna Guy whose work was influenced by her; either way the authenticity of the dances must be questioned. (St Denis, who began her career as a chorus girl, was initially inspired to create her exotic dances by the picture of an Egyptian goddess on a cigarette poster.) The group of dances that Guy performed to Negro spirituals seemed to have pleased the critics better as being drawn from a more recognisable and ethnically genuine source.

Winfield's own solo, Bronze Study, was criticised by John Martin, the influential critic of the *New York Times*, as having 'proved to be merely the exhibition of an exemplary physique'. In his review Martin referred to the company's performance as 'the oustanding novelty of the season', an indication of how seriously he regarded the occasion.

It is doubtful if Winfield and his colleagues had made any anthropological study of African dance forms – where, indeed, could they do so without travelling to the Caribbean or to Africa itself – but their attempts to depict Black dance in a serious manner, however eclectic or lacking in authenticity, at least represented Afro-American dance as rooted in a culture that expressed itself in movement far removed from the frivolities of the dance hall and vaudeville theatre. Black concert dance was struggling to be born; authenticity would come later.

Winfield himself was concerned with what has been called the 'Black aesthetic' in dance. The period in which he was creating dances for his company is referred to as the Harlem Renaissance – an era when there was a Black movement in the arts, in poetry, drama, literature and music, and dance was no exception. In October 1933, after a dance performance led by Winfield at the Harlem YWCA on 138th Street, he took part in a forum which considered the question: 'What shall the Negro dance about?' It was a question and a challenge that has concerned Black dancers and choreographers ever since, but in today's climate the Black artist feels freer either to confront the question or to ignore it as he wishes.

In 1933 Winfield's company appeared in Hall Johnson's play *Run Lil Chillun*, which had choreography by Doris Humphrey – rather an odd choice, as Humphrey had evolved a personal vocabulary of movement that was abstract in style and deliberately eschewed emotion as an element in dance. That same year Winfield directed the dance sequences in Louis Gruenberg's opera *The Emperor Jones*, based on the play by Eugene O'Neill. The management wanted the opera chorus and dancers to appear in Black-face rather than use Winfield's Black company, but the leading singer Laurence Tibbett refused to go on unless Winfield's group appeared. The management responded by not listing the dancers in the programme. Winfield danced the role of the Witch Doctor, thus becoming the first Black dancer to appear at the Metropolitan Opera. He was still performing the role when he died suddenly from pneumonia in 1934. His obituary in the *New York Herald-Tribune* commented on his 'savage dances amid jungle scenes of Voodoo', raising the question of what sources, if any, he had used in choreographing the role.

Winfield's premature death robbed Black dance of one of its most enterprising artists, a man whose attempts to present Afro-American dance as a subject for serious consideration paved the way for other pioneers in concert dance. Winfield's final words were: 'We're building a foundation that will make people take Black dance seriously.'

In the same year that Winfield died, Asadata Dafora (he also used the surname Horton because his great-grandfather had been taken as a slave to Nova Scotia and had adopted the surname of his owner) created a sensation in New York with his full-length production of *Kykunkor (The Witch Woman)*.

Dafora was born in Sierra Leone and arrived in New York in 1929, having studied music in Europe. *Kykunkor*, produced at the Little Theater on West 44th Street, was a tremendous success both with critics and audiences, and it is interesting to speculate whether it would have had the same reception had it been conceived by Winfield or one of his Afro-American colleagues. As it was, *Kykunkor* had a mixed cast of Africans and Afro-Americans, assembled by Francis Atkins of Winfield's company. The story concerned a curse placed on a bridegroom (Dafora) and the attempts to remove it.

Unlike concert dance performances that preceded it, *Kykunkor* had an interesting narrative with its various dances threaded through the story: there were dances for the witch doctor, dances of joy and celebration, a challenge dance, a war dance, a jester dance and a festival dance – each one of which had its part to play in telling the story, and each one representative of an aspect of a tribal community in which dance played an important part of everyday life. *Kykunkor* presented real human beings not caricatures, and it told its story in an exciting way, with the addition of African instrumental and vocal music. As a theatrical production it pointed in the direction that Katherine Dunham was to take with her Caribbean dance narratives.

► *Asadata Dafora as the bridegroom in his production of* Kykunkor, *presented in New York City in 1934. Dafora was one of the pioneers of Black concert dance.*

But if *Kykunkor* established that Black dance was a theatrical force that could be taken seriously, it also reinforced the fallacious idea that Black artists were restricted to certain thematic formulae. John Martin, reviewing *Kykunkor*, acknowledged that it was 'a revelation of the possibilities of the field', but he went on to state that: 'Negroes cannot be expected to do dances designed for another race.' It would be some time before Black artists broke through the barriers erected by such thinking.

In 1938 Dafora produced another major work *Zunguru*, which, although it was considered to be a better production than *Kykunkor*, failed to have the same impact; even though the distinguished critic Walter Terry wrote that it contained 'the wildest dancing you ever saw'. By then, of course, such second generation pioneers of modern dance as Doris Humphrey, Charles Weidman and Martha Graham had startled the dance world with works like Humphrey's *With My Red Fires*, the Lynch Town episode of Weidman's *Atavisms*, and a whole string of innovative Graham works, from *Primitive Mysteries* (1931), to *Frontier* (1935) and *American Document* (1938). At that time the *avant garde* world of modern dance was creating such a stir that the attempts of Black dancers and choreographers to be taken seriously – even to be part of that movement – were overlooked and overshadowed.

Portents of what was to come, however, could be seen – for those who cared to look – in a programme presented at the 92nd Street YMHA entitled Negro Dance Evening. The programme included Edna Guy performing some of her dances based on spirituals, Asadata Dafora and some members of his company, and a newcomer to the New York dance scene, Katherine Dunham, performing several Haitian ceremonial dances. Another of the dancers was Talley Beatty, a dancer/choreographer who was destined to be amongst the most important Black artists who would break the barriers and taboos that had surrounded Afro-Americans for so long.

20

New Movements

Throughout the thirties new forms of dance developed and flourished in Europe and America. In Germany particularly there was a new Expressionist movement, headed by Rudolf von Laban, Kurt Jooss, Mary Wigman and Hanya Holm; and in America there were Doris Humphrey, Charles Weidman and Martha Graham, later joined by Holm who was sent to America to open a branch of the Wigman school and afterwards started her own studio in New York.

All these innovative dancer/choreographers were experimenting with new forms of movement developed from a personal aesthetic, but, while they differed in style and idiom, they were all concerned with dance as an expressive form of theatre.

At the same time there were a number of Black dancer/choreographers working with the same purpose except that, instead of struggling to evolve a whole new vocabulary of movement, many of them were building on a cultural heritage of dance that went back untold centuries. Most of it, rooted in African tribal dance, was remote; some of it was more accessible, hitherto used only for popular entertainment.

Asadata Dafora, coming from Sierra Leone, had proved with *Kykunkor* that there was an audience for Black narrative dance. Hemsley Winfield, Edna Guy and their associates in the New Negro Art Dancers company had also established that concert dance, based on Afro-American themes, was a viable proposition. On University campuses there was a parallel movement to establish Black dance as a serious venture.

At the Negro College, Hampton Institute in Hampton, Virginia, the Creative Dance Group was formed under the leadership of Charles H. Williams, the director of physical education at Hampton. The Group gave recitals throughout the country, performing a wide variety of dances based on African tribal customs. Some of these were formulated by Williams, based on anthropological treatises, others were mounted by students from overseas.

A number of the dances were reconstructed directly from African tribal material, such as Mamah Parah, which was danced on stilts: Wyomamie, a dance based on African marriage ceremonies; and the Fangai Man, which dealt with witchcraft, rather in the manner of the West Indian Obeah religion.

The Creative Dance Group also revived the old plantation dances, such as the Juba and the Cake Walk, not in their sophisticated minstrel forms, but as they were originally done in the more ingenuous Saturday night frolics in front of the Big House. The group essayed a performance of a piece entitled *Middle Passage*, a dance narrative enacting the horrors of the slave trade; and performed dances based on Negro spirituals similar to those created by Edna Guy. Unfortunately, although the Creative Dance Group received some critical comment – most of it complimentary – none of the writers made comparisons with Guy's work so that we cannot tell what relative qualities they possessed.

Although the performances by the Creative Dance Group were amateur, their influence in disseminating an awareness of the Black dance heritage was considerable. Many of the students who participated were majoring in physical education and would be teaching in segregated schools throughout America. Their potential in creating new programmes of Black dance, and in building knowledgeable audiences for the future, was considerable.

Hampton was not the only college where Black dance groups were formed: similar concert dance companies were created in several segregated institutions in the south, including Spellman College in Atlanta, Fisk University, Howard University and Tuskegee Institute.

The campus activity and the various concert performances in New York and elsewhere created a psychological climate in which Black dance could evolve in its more serious, expressive forms. Like so many aesthetic movements in many cultures throughout the world, there seemed to be a sudden gathering of ideas, almost as if there were artistic organisms born on the wind, spreading throughout the Black communities in the big cities of America, a growing creative force led by a number of seminal figures who were to become famous not just in the areas of Black dance, but as leaders in the new movements that were developing in the western world.

21

Pearl Primus

Pearl Primus was amongst the first, and certainly one of the most important, of the dancer/choreographers who gave Black concert dance a new impetus during the 1940s.

Primus was born in Trinidad in 1919, and moved to New York with her parents when she was two years old. She majored in biology and pre-medicine at Hunter College, graduating in 1940. She entered graduate school and while trying to find a day-time job she approached the National Youth Administration for assistance. Unable to find her the sort of work she wanted she was placed in an NYA dance group as an understudy. Her progress, through natural ability, was so rapid that she auditioned for, and won, a scholarship with the New Dance Group.

The New Dance Group was formed during the Depression in 1932 as a kind of dancers' collective, pooling resources and working as a number of individuals and groups sharing a single programme or series of performances, and holding informal discussions and forums on the direction of modern dance at a time when the art was in considerable ferment.

Primus worked and studied at the New Dance Group school, concentrating on various forms of 'primitive' dance – a series of researches that acted as an antidote to the 'wounds inflicted by racial discrimination'. After six months research she completed her first work, *African Ceremonial*, a solo that she performed in front of African friends so that they could comment on its authenticity.

Her first professional appearance was on February 14, 1943, at the YMHA on Lexington Avenue and 92nd Street, during which she danced in a number of works of her own, including *African Ceremonial*, *Strange Fruit* and *Hard Time Blues*. These two last works were both dances of protest: *Strange Fruit* being the reaction to the lynching of a Black man, and *Hard Time Blues* a protest against sharecropping (the practice whereby a farmer was forced to share the return of his crops or produce with his landlord). Primus' concern with African dance was primarily

◄ *Pearl Primus who,
together with Katherine
Dunham, was one of the
most important Black
anthropologist/dancer/
teacher/choreographers
of this century.*

anthropological; her concern with the Afro-American was with the racial oppression he suffered.

Primus' debut at the YMHA was shared with four other dancers. The critic John Martin afterwards wrote of Primus that: 'If ever a young dancer was entitled to a company of her own and the freedom to do what she chooses with it, she is it.' Martin's sympathetic review encouraged Primus to ask his advice and on the basis of this she began – or rather, continued – her serious study of dance.

Her next engagement however was not so serious. She was invited to perform as an entertainer in a nightclub called Cafe Society Downtown, and while her performances there were highly professional and the money she earned was useful, it was not what she wanted to do. After ten months she left to continue her studies, to teach at the New Dance Group and to prepare for her first solo concert performance.

One of her ways of preparation was to travel extensively in the deep south throughout the summer of 1944, visiting nearly seventy Negro churches to study their ceremonials, and living and picking cotton with the sharecroppers. This first-hand experience of the segregated lifestyle of Black people in the southern states, their work, hopes, religious beliefs, ways and means of relaxation, was invaluable material for her choreographic themes which, while accurately based on the movement motifs of Afro-Americans, embodied thematic ideas of protest against their oppression.

Primus' Broadway debut took place at the Belasco Theater, on October 4, 1944. This concert performance included two of her previous successes, *Strange Fruit* and *Hard Time Blues*, as well as *African Ceremonial* and *Yonvaloo*, which was based on a dance of Haitian origin. One of the greatest successes of that performance was a work entitled *The Negro Speaks of Rivers*, based on a poem by Langston Hughes.

The critic of the *Daily Worker*, Edith Segal, afterwards wrote that: 'Miss Primus has wisely gone to the rich heritage of her people and has brought us treasures of great beauty, enhanced by her own enormous talent. Pearl Primus reaches her greatest moments in her dances of protest.'

Following this success Primus expanded her company, which next appeared at the Roxy Theater the following December. For this appearance she re-choreographed *African Ceremonial* as a group work which John Martin called 'definitely and legitimately exciting'. Such concert appearances could not of course provide the necessary income to sustain her and once more she resorted to the commercial theatre, dancing in a revival of *Showboat* while at the same time preparing and performing several more concert recitals.

In 1947 Ruth Page, the ballerina, choreographer and dance director, much of whose work was centred on Chicago, invited Primus to dance the Hemsley Winfield role of the Witch Doctor in a revival of *The Emperor Jones* in that city.

A year later, while performing a number of her reconstructed African dances at a concert performance at Fisk University, Primus was seen by the President of the Rosenwald Foundation, Dr Edwin Embree. He was surprised to discover that Primus had never been to Africa and he arranged that she should be granted a Rosenwald Fellowship. As a result Primus was able to travel, study and perform in Africa, visiting the Gold Coast, Angola, the Cameroons, Liberia, Senegal and what was then the Belgian Congo during a trip lasting eighteen months.

Throughout her journey she studied and participated in the native African dances and also performed her own; both she and her work were enthusiastically accepted by all the Africans she met and she was 'adopted' by the Nigerians who named her Omowale, meaning 'child returned home'. This African journey was a tremendous emotional and aesthetic experience for Primus, and her work gained a new strength and authority from it.

Just how important the experience had been was apparent at a concert performance she gave at the American Museum of Natural History in May 1952. The programme included such new works as *Impinyuze*, a dance from the Belgian Congo; *Dance of Strength* from Sierra Leone, and dances from Liberia and Nigeria performed under the title *Excerpts from an African Journey*.

In 1953 Primus spent the summer studying dances of the West Indies. It was during this visit that she met Percival Borde whom she subsequently married. Like Primus, Borde was born in Trinidad, a dancer, choreographer, teacher, and lecturer who had made a great study of the dance forms of the Caribbean and their African origins.

In 1958 Primus appeared as a guest artist with Borde's own troupe, receiving enthusiastic reviews for her performance of a dance of welcome, *Fanga*, joyous in manner and demanding virtuosity in its execution, requiring a 'shimmering flow of waist and hips that makes the dancer seem almost boneless.'

In 1959 Primus returned to Africa and was appointed Director of Liberia's Performing Arts Centre. Her brief was 'to discover, restore, revive and expand African dance and allied cultures'. After a brief return to the United States following two years in Liberia, Primus and Borde both went to Africa again, this time under the aegis of the Rebecca Harkness Foundation.

Between a number of trips to Africa Primus and Borde opened the

▲ *Pearl Primus (second left) with members of her company.*

Primus-Borde School of Primal Dance in New york City. Primus not only taught dance but lectured on anthropology and sociology. Later she taught at her *alma mater*, Hunter College. She also became closely involved with lecturing and teaching in Harlem and Newark.

Primus' contribution to Afro-American dance culture was immense, both in her anthropological investigations and in her use of Afro-Caribbean movement as a form of protest against the many forms of oppression that Black Americans have suffered under the segregation laws. She presented her work with an effective directness, never adding a meretricious glamour but with a stagecraft that emphasised the strength, dignity, pride and virtuosity inherent in the various forms of Black dance. Primus was a pioneer who did much to break down the stereotyped image of the Negro, both African and American, and resurrected him as a human being possessed of a culture that can be shared as part of the heritage of every American.

In a magazine interview in 1968 Primus said, 'I dance not to entertain but to help people better understand each other.... Because through dance I have experienced the wordless joy of freedom, I seek it more fully now for my people and for all people everywhere.'

22

Katherine Dunham

There are both fundamental similarities and fundamental differences in the work and careers of Pearl Primus and Katherine Dunham: they are different sides of the same coin. Whereas Primus allowed her dances to make their own statement – a statement made strong by the vitality and beauty of her own performances – Dunham presented hers with all the forces of modern theatre as emphasis: dramatic lighting, brilliant costumes, lavish settings. Yet her dances were as authentic as Primus', equally rooted in the culture they so vibrantly celebrated.

Dunham was born in Chicago in 1912, seven years before Primus, and discovered the pleasures of dance in High School, where she excelled in athletics. Getting good grades and working hard to support herself, Dunham entered the University of Chicago where she studied anthropology. She also took dance classes with Mark Turbyfill, a ballet teacher, and Ludmila Speranzeva, who taught modern dance. Through Turbyfill Dunham met Ruth Page who at that time was ballet mistress at the Chicago Civic Opera, and it was in Ruth Page's ballet *La Guiablesse*, based on West Indian themes, that Dunham made her professional debut in 1933.

At this time Dunham had opened her own small dance school which helped to pay for her anthropological studies at the university. She also choreographed works for the Cube Theater Club which she had established with her brother Albert, who was six years older than her, and a Greek student Nicolas Matsukas. At one of these performances Dunham was seen by Mrs Alfred Rosenwald Stern of the Rosenwald Foundation who, together with the psychoanalyst Erich Fromm, was instrumental in Dunham being awarded a Travel Fellowship to pursue her anthropological dance studies in the West Indies. When Dunham was interviewed by board members of the Rosenwald Foundation, she performed an impromptu dance of vaguely Voodoo origin that so astonished the board that they were immediately convinced of her theories about the relationship between anthropology and dance.

▶ *Katherine Dunham, dancer/choreographer/ teacher/anthropologist, one of the most important and influential pioneers of Black dance in the twentieth century, whose company had a world-wide success in the 1950s.*

Dunham arrived in the Caribbean in 1936 and studied the various regional dance forms in Martinique, Jamaica, Trinidad, and in particular Haiti. The very fact that a relatively poor Black girl from Chicago was conducting the first anthropological field studies of West Indian dances was in itself an extraordinary achievement at that time.

The fact that Dunham was Black herself and could dance – quickly picking up the various steps, although amazed to find her stamina was no match for the apparently inexhaustible dancers of Jamaica – was a great advantage. Even so, she found in Haiti that there was a strong caste system founded on skin colour, with mulattos the social elite, rather as they had been in New Orleans during the latter part of the eighteenth century. But Dunham's own physical beauty, her natural grace and sensitivity, enabled her to break down a number of barriers and carry out her studies at first hand, laying the groundwork for continuing research and performance.

Not long after her return from the Caribbean Dunham was invited to take part in the inaugural programme of the New York YMHA series, the Negro Dance Evening, in 1937. This performance was instrumental in Dunham being invited to become Dance Director of the Chicago branch of the Federal Theater Project for which she staged *L'Ag'Ya*, a Martinique fighting dance set in a fishing village. Dunham wrote the scenario, choreographed, produced and performed in the piece with a predominantly amateur cast.

When the Federal Theater Project closed in 1939 Dunham persuaded the owner of the Sherman Hotel in Chicago to accept her and her company alongside Duke Ellington and his band as part of the floor-show. Dunham produced some strong cabaret-style dances based on Afro-American themes such as Barrelhouse, a raunchy jazz number, and the ever popular Cake Walk. She also proposed a couple of more ethnic dances, Rara Tonga and Bolero, to be danced barefoot; Ernest Byfield the owner/Director was uncertain that his elegant clientele would accept such 'primitive' dances but he took a chance and Dunham and her company were a great success. This ability to synthesise genuine ethnic dance with unabashed show-business theatricality was to be developed with sensational success in years to come.

That same year Dunham was made Director of the New York Labor Stage where she choreographed a musical called *Pins and Needles*. With the money she earned she was able to support nine members of her company whom she had brought from Chicago.

With this company Dunham produced a concert at the Windsor Theater that was the foundation of her subsequent success as the Director of a Black company possessed of an exhilarating and exciting repertoire.

The concert was given the deliberately enticing title *Tropics and Le Jazz Hot*, and was scheduled for one night only on February 18, 1940. It achieved such popular acclaim that it ran for thirteen consecutive Sundays garnering enthusiastic reviews from John Martin and Walter Terry and establishing Dunham as the most potent new force in Black dance.

The suite *Le Jazz Hot* was divided into three sections; the second section, that same 'Barrelhouse (Florida Swamp Shimmy)', was described by Martin as 'a truly wonderful little genre piece'. It was a seemingly impromptu dance, suggested by the involuntary dances that took place in the many barrelhouses, or drinking dens, that abounded in the Black neighbourhoods of most big American cities. These establishments often hosted some of the finest jazz bands of the time, especially in New Orleans and Chicago, and their playing frequently moved the listeners to dance to the infectious rhythms; Dunham's dance epitomised these performances, sometimes exuberant, sometimes melancholy – if the jazzmen were playing blues – and often sexy.

In the section known as 'Tropics – Shore Excursion', Dunham danced the role of the Woman with the Cigar, another genre piece in which she displayed her strong, provocative stage presence.

That same year Dunham and her troupe appeared in the musical *Cabin in the Sky* which starred Ethel Waters, with Dunham playing the part of the seductive Georgia Browne in a story about a gambler who is reformed by a dream of his own death.

From Broadway Dunham went to Hollywood to appear in the first of several films, *Star-Spangled Rhythm*, one of those war-time Hollywood films in which the studios, in this case Paramount, presented most of the stars on their payroll in some flimsy story.

At this time Dunham had met the stage designer and painter John Pratt, a white man born in Canada to American parents, who was subsequently to become her husband. Pratt was responsible for the design of all of Dunham's productions, including several of her films.

In 1943 Dunham appeared in the film version of *Cabin in the Sky* (MGM). That same year the Dunham company appeared in the all-Black film *Stormy Weather* (TCF), a revue that took the life story of Bill 'Bojangles' Robinson as its theme, and starred Robinson, The Nicholas Brothers, Lena Horne, Cab Calloway and Fats Waller.

With such Hollywood successes – and the money they provided – Dunham was able to expand her company and its repertoire, and of course the publicity received from the films now made the company known across the country and beyond.

In September 1943 Dunham's company opened at New York's

▲ *(Left) Katherine Dunham in a scene from the film* Cabin in the Sky. *(Right) Katherine Dunham in one of her most successful works* L'ag 'ya.

Martin Beck Theater in a new production *Tropical Revue*. With attractive decors by Pratt, the show included some of Dunham's proven favourites such as 'Shore Excursion' and numbers from *Le Jazz Hot*, as well as a suite of dances taken from a work entitled *Br'er Rabbit* about which the critics had been less than enthusiastic; the suite was called 'Plantation Dances' and included a Cake Walk, Juba, Pas Mala, Ballin' the Jack and Strut – all the favourites from the minstrel days and shows like *Shuffle Along*.

Tropical Revue included one new big work 'Rites de Passage'. In four parts, it portrayed four types of ritual: Puberty, Fertility, Death, and Women's Mysteries. The work had undisguised qualities of sexuality, especially in the fertility section, which excited audiences and led to the work being banned in Boston. Nevertheless it was a great success and was a perfect example of Dunham's flair for taking genuine ethnic dance and giving it tremendous theatrical vitality. At this point in her career there is no doubt that Dunham and her company represented Black dance at its most potent and appealing.

In 1945 Dunham's company opened in a musical play *Carib Song*, which was not well received by the critics but which included a new work 'Shango', which was considered one of Dunham's best pieces of choreography. In the piece, which had Voodoo associations, an initiate was splashed with the blood of a chicken and believed himself possessed by a snake spirit, the dancer writhing serpent-like in an apparent trance.

That same year Dunham opened her School of Dance at 220 West 43rd Street. As early as 1938, after she had established her small school in Chicago, Dunham had stated that her intentions were: 'To establish a well-trained ballet group. To develop a technique that will be as important to the white man as to the Negro. To attain a status in the dance world that will give to the Negro dance student the courage really to study, and a reason to do so. And to take *our* dance out of the burlesque – to make it a more dignified art.'

Some of these aspirations had already been achieved by Dunham's company. Now her new school was in a position to pass on and con-solidate much that the company had achieved. In addition to a full curriculum of dance and theatre subjects, Dunham's school was unique in offering classes in philosophy, French, Spanish, West Indian folk culture, music appreciation and reading. This wide-ranging curriculum was devised because Dunham's experience in forming a company had taught her that many young artists had been handicapped by a general lack of understanding of a cultural history of any sort and its importance in a specific field. The dance technique that was taught was a com-bination of classical ballet with Central European, Caribbean and African elements – it was nothing if not eclectic and ensured that the students would have a training that would allow them to follow dance careers in a multiplicity of disciplines.

The Dunham school remained in existence until 1955 and during its ten years it did much to influence a generation of young American dancers, whatever the colour of their skins.

In 1946 Dunham produced another revue-like show *Bal Nègre*, which was considered by the critics to be superior to her previous shows, having 'a new dignity ... a new taste'. Amongst this company was a young artist destined to become a world celebrity – Eartha Kitt. During the next few years Dunham's company toured the world, achiev-ing what can only be called a sensational success in Europe, particularly in Britain and France.

In 1962 Dunham produced a new show *Bamboche*, which was notable for the fact that it incorporated authentic Moroccan village dancers in the production. It was not a great success – the Bay of Pigs debacle kept people glued to their television screens and away from the theatre.

Dunham's last performance – unannounced as such – took place appropriately at Harlem's Apollo Theater in 1965. In a sense it was a release: the years of struggling to keep her company going and her dancers in work were over; now she was free to write, to lecture, to teach. During 1966 she became Cultural Adviser to both the President and the Minister of Cultural Affairs in Dakar, Senegal.

Dunham returned to East St Louis in 1967, where at Southern Illinois University she established her Cultural Arts Programme, which included three community centres and a small performance group, a salutary beacon of hope in an area where there is much illiteracy amongst the local Black population, with many students dropping out of school before the age of sixteen, and where poverty and deprivation are a major social problem.

In 1987 the Alvin Ailey American Dance Theatre undertook the reconstruction, documentation and performance of a number of Dunham works, including *L'Ag'Ya*, *Shango*, and a suite of dances such as 'Flaming Youth' and 'Barrelhouse (Florida Swamp Shimmy)'. The original costumes and scenery were renovated and restored and the works have been integrated into the Ailey company repertoire, so that some of the best of Dunham's works are preserved as a legacy for future generations to enjoy.

23

Alvin Ailey

Alvin Ailey bestrides the Black dance scene if not like a colossus at least as a figure who has presented it on a scale and with a seriousness that matches the achievements of many white companies. But perhaps his greatest importance lies in having created a synthesis between Black and white dance forms that reveals the possibility of a happy co-existence in which one can gain strength from the other: Black themes are presented within the disciplines of white movement vocabularies. Black vitality and rhythmic complexities contribute powerful dynamics to white formal structures. And it all adds up to splendid, exuberant – and frequently moving – dance theatre.

Ailey was born in Rogers, Texas, in 1931, moving to Los Angeles in his youth. Attending the Jefferson High School he participated in athletics before graduating in 1948 and enrolling in UCLA (University of California at Los Angeles) to study Romance languages. He transferred to Los Angeles City College and in 1951 went to San Francisco State College. Two years earlier he had made the acquaintance of the Lester Horton Dance Theatre (Horton organised the first multi-racial modern company in the USA) working as part of the stage crew. He made his debut as a dancer with the company in 1953, appearing in a revue entitled *Bel Caribe*. Horton died that same year and Ailey briefly took over the direction of the company.

In 1954 he was invited to appear at the prestigious Jacob's Pillow Dance Festival and he also danced in the film *Carmen Jones* (TCF), a Black updating of Bizet's opera *Carmen*, starring Dorothy Dandridge, Harry Belafonte and Pearl Bailey. The choreographer of the film, Herbert Ross, remembered Ailey's dancing and together with another dancer from the Horton company, Carmen de Lavallade, invited him to appear on Broadway in the new musical *House of Flowers*. Despite an attractive score, book by Truman Capote and decor by Oliver Messel, the musical only ran for four months, but Ailey made great use of his stay in New York, continuing his dance training with such major

◄ *The Alvin Ailey Company in* Revelations, *one of his most famous and popular works based on Negro spirituals, blues and gospel songs.*

innovators and teachers as Martha Graham, Hanya Holm, Doris Humphrey, Anna Sokolow and Karel Shook.

During the years 1954–8 Ailey danced in several musicals on and off Broadway, including *The Carefree Tree*, Harry Belafonte's *Sing, Man Sing* in which he partnered Mary Hinkson, one of Martha Graham's most prominent soloists, and he was the leading dancer in *Jamaica* which starred Lena Horne. During these years he also danced with Anna Sokolow, Sophie Maslow and his contemporary Donald McKayle. Ailey's first concert performance was at the YMHA on 92nd Street, the same year and the same venue as the first performance by the Alvin Ailey American Dance Theatre.

Ailey received much praise from the critics for his abilities as a dancer, his good looks and his fine physique supported by a strong, wide-ranging technique. The critic John Martin wrote that: 'he is strikingly handsome, with the genuine theatre artist's inborn power of projection. His technique is strong and his quality of movement is notably beautiful, like that of a svelte, nervously alert animal.'

Ailey's company received similarly enthusiastic reviews from its inception and rapidly established itself as one of the most important American modern dance companies – with, of course, a predominantly Black cast and a repertoire reflecting Black themes. While the company is fully integrated – it has always had a multi-racial composition – Ailey has said that, 'I feel an obligation to use Black dancers because there must be more opportunities for them but *not* because I am a Black choreographer talking to Black people.'

Ailey's choreography has ranged as widely as his own training and abilities, with many of his works becoming modern classics. Apart from what is usually described, for want of a more exact word, as 'jazz' dance, Ailey has rarely used the more immediately recognisable Black dance forms such as the Juba, the Cake Walk or any of the 'bird dances' such as the Turkey Strut or Buzzard Lope. Even one of his greatest and most enduring works *Revelations*, which is based on Negro spirituals, is more abstract in movement, although the music itself and the intensity and rhythmic force with which it is always interpreted provide an atmosphere, a mood, instantly associated with the travails of the Afro-American in the deep south throughout three centuries. Even so, *Revelations* transcends any specific time and place and achieves a universal expression of the spirit of mankind. The critic Arthur Todd described the work as 'one of the most beautifully constructed and moving works in the repertory of any company.'

Ailey's eclectic choice of styles has included several pure jazz works, such as *Blues Suite*, created to traditional jazz in 1958 and still in the

▲ Alvin Ailey, one of the most important forces in integrating Black and white dancers.

company repertoire; *Roots of the Blues*, also traditional; and *Night Creature*, to the score of that name by Duke Ellington. His most recent jazz piece is *For Bird with Love*, to music by Charles 'Bird' Parker, 'Dizzy' Gillespie, Count Basie and Jerome Kern.

Two of Ailey's most prominent dancers, the statuesque Judith Jamison and the strong but sensitive Dudley Williams, inspired two wonderful solos: *Cry*, for Jamison, is a work 'dedicated to and about the fortitude of Black women, especially our mothers', and *Love Songs*, for Williams, revealed a number of emotions from physical passion to fear and pathos.

Other works by Ailey range from the big company display piece *Caverna Magica*, which explores the mystical and magical elements in the Black ethos, to a lyrical, pastoral work like *The Lark Ascending*, to the score by Ralph Vaughan Williams. In addition to a huge canon of works created for his own company, Ailey has choreographed for such major classical ballet companies as American Ballet Theatre, the Joffrey Ballet, the Paris Opera Ballet, London Festival Ballet and the Royal Danish Ballet.

It has been Ailey's policy to invite many choreographers to create for his company, including Hans van Manen, Talley Beatty, Bill T. Jones and Arnie Zane, Jennifer Muller, Judith Jamison, Donald McKayle and Ulysses Dove, thus ensuring a wide appeal to audiences and obviating the danger of the company becoming merely a 'working museum' for Ailey choreography when he is no longer there.

Since its creation in 1958 the Alvin Ailey American Dance Theater has performed for an estimated number of over fifteen million people in forty-eight States of America, forty-five countries and on six continents. The company's extensive touring commitments began in 1962 with a tour to the Far East, South-East Asia and Australia sponsored by the US State Department. Since then there have been more than twenty-five international tours, the most spectacularly successful being, perhaps, the tour of Soviet Russia in 1970 – the first American modern dance company to visit the USSR since the days of Isadora Duncan. In 1985 the company undertook the first government-sponsored tour of the People's Republic of China since the restoration of Sino-American relations.

Another major achievement of the Alvin Ailey American Dance Theater was the pioneering of long-term residency programmes established by the National Endowment for the Arts. The first residency was held in Atlanta, Georgia, in 1977, and the second in Los Angeles in 1983. Sponsored by the Kansas City Friends of Alvin Ailey, the company performed two long residencies in Kansas City, Missouri, in 1984 and 1986.

The Alvin Ailey Dance Theater Foundation administers the Alvin Ailey American Dance Center at 1515 Broadway, New York, a school for dance training, as well as the Alvin Ailey Repertory Ensemble, the junior resident company of the school. Through his own dynamic dancing, his prolific choreography, the world-wide touring of his company and the continuing work of the school, Ailey has made an incalculable contribution to American dance in general and to Black dance in particular.

24

Donald McKayle

In some ways Donald McKayle is to Alvin Ailey what Pearl Primus was
to Katherine Dunham; working on a smaller scale and somewhat more
directly – although it would be wrong to push the analogy much further.
While Ailey ranged widely in his choreographic themes, McKayle has
remained more immediately concerned with the human condition.
Sometimes that concern has been with specifically Black themes, more
often it is with all mankind. The British-born critic P. W. Manchester
who later edited the magazine *Dance News* in New York and became
Visiting Professor at the North Carolina School of the Arts, wrote of
him: 'All his best works deal, not with abstractions, but with people;
living, laughing, suffering, bitter, pitiful, protesting, superbly human
beings.' Of his own works McKayle wrote that: 'they are not limited
to nor do they necessarily exclude Negro source material.'

McKayle was born in 1930 in New York, and it was a performance
by Pearl Primus that first excited him about the dramatic possibilities of
dance. During his last year at high school he auditioned for and was
granted a year's scholarship to the New Dance Group – just as Primus
had done. He studied with Primus, Sophie Maslow, William Bales and
Jean Erdman, and also enrolled in New York City College. He made
his dance debut in 1948 – some five years before his close contemporary,
Ailey – at the Mansfield Theatre in works by Maslow and Erdman.

His ability as a dancer won McKayle a scholarship to the Martha
Graham school and during 1955–6 he danced with her company during
its Far Eastern tour. He performed as a guest artist with the companies
of Anna Sokolow and Merce Cunningham, with the result that his early
career as a dancer was involved with some of the greatest gurus and
most *avant garde* artists working in modern dance.

Other dance activities included performing in Charles Weidman's
Traditions, performing with the Dudley-Maslow-Bales troupe and
appearing as soloist with the New York City Opera Company. But like
so many dancers – Black and white – dancing with 'serious' or concert

companies provided little income; McKayle found it necessary to appear in the more commercial world of musical shows. One of his first appearances on Broadway was in *Bless You All* choreographed by Helen Tamiris, and then, like Ailey, he danced in *House of Flowers*. He later became dance captain in *West Side Story* and this experience served him well when, during the next decade, he choreographed several musicals.

Together with a number of other choreographers, including Daniel Nagrin who had co-choreographed *Bless You All* with Tamiris, McKayle formed the Contemporary Dance Group. Although the enterprise met with little success, Nagrin and McKayle combined talents to present a concert of modern dance at Hunter College in 1951, and it was on this occasion that McKayle's classic work *Games* was first produced.

The piece was concerned with children's street games, the sort of games, both traditional and improvised, that children play in all big cities around the world but in this case directly recalled by the choreographer's own childhood experiences. In an article McKayle wrote:

> It was a childhood memory that triggered my first dance. ... It was dusk, and the block was dimly lit by a street lamp around which we hovered choosing a game. The street, playground of tenement children, was soon ringing with calls and cries, the happy shouts of the young. The street lamp threw a shadow large and looming – the constant spectre of fear – 'Chickee the Cop!' The cry was broken; the game became a sordid dance of terror.

Of course the dancers McKayle used were not children – not even very young dancers – but his imaginative choreography, without resorting to the sort of stereotyped movements so often seen when adults imitate the actions of the young, created the impression of watching children, their energy and their total ability to immerse themselves in fantasy.

After *Games* McKayle produced a number of other works of some consequence, mostly abstract, but in 1959 came *Rainbow 'Round My Shoulder,* incontrovertibly a dance of protest if not specifically concerned with a Black theme, and inspired by the chain gangs of southern convicts, many of whom were in fact Black. Danced to traditional prison songs, the work dealt with the convicts' dreams of freedom and family, particularly the women from whom they were separated; mothers, sweethearts and wives. It was a work with tremendous dramatic impact, full of anger and sadness but never sentimental, and reflecting McKayle's concern with the human – or in this case, inhuman – condition.

In lighter vein, McKayle created *District Storyville* in 1962, a work based on New Orleans jazz, and he used jazz again for another work with a contemporary theme, *Reflections in the Park*, a picture of New York street life.

Throughout the sixties and seventies McKayle was in great demand as a choreographer of musicals, television shows and films. He staged the dances for *Golden Boy* starring Sammy Davis, and choreographed Harry Belafonte's television specials *The Strollin' Twenties*. He also

◄ Donald McKayle with Carmen de Lavallade (wife of Geoffrey Holder) in one of his most beautiful and moving works, Rainbow 'Round My Shoulder.

choreographed the film version of *The Great White Hope*, a thinly disguised biography of the black boxer Jack Johnson, starring James Earl Jones. McKayle also choreographed the Disney Studio's *Bedknobs and Broomsticks* and the last of several remakes of *The Jazz Singer*.

Throughout his career McKayle has also been in great demand as a teacher of modern dance, working in New York, London, Tel Aviv, Cologne and Tunis. More recently he has been associated with the repertory dance group at the Los Angeles Inner City Cultural Center and was appointed Artistic Director of the School of Dance, California Institute of Arts, in 1975.

Together with his contempories, Alvin Ailey and Talley Beatty, Donald McKayle has been largely responsible for breaking down the stereotyped image of the Black dancer and has done an enormous amount, in his dancing, his choreography, his teaching and his writing, not just to make the Black dancer acceptable in what is still a white-dominated art form, but also, happily, an ever increasing, commonplace figure.

25

Talley Beatty

With training that encompassed ballet, modern dance, ethnic and jazz, Talley Beatty rivals Alvin Ailey in the range and experience of his dance background.

Born in 1923, a member of a large Louisiana family, Beatty's genetic history is equally mixed, having an amalgam of Afro-Caribbean, Cajun-Indian, Creole and white blood. Yet, for all this considerable artistic and racial complexity, it is the Black experience, either in Afro-Caribbean or big-city streetwise mode, that surfaces most often and most successfully.

Beatty began his dance career in Ruth Page's production of *La Guiablesse* for the Chicago Civic Opera. Two years later he was one of the original nine dancers who travelled with Katherine Dunham from Chicago to New York in 1937, to appear at the 92nd Street YMHA's Negro Dance Evening that included such formative artists as Edna Guy and Asadata Dafora. In that concert Beatty danced the role of a priest in Dunham's *Yonvalou*, was the central dancer in *Carnival Dances*, and starred as the fugitive in *Swamp Suite*. Three years later he returned to New York with Dunham to take leading roles in *Le Jazz Hot*. He also appeared in several Broadway shows that Dunham choreographed, including *Cabin in the Sky, Pins and Needles* and *Blue Holiday*.

During his early twenties Beatty studied at the School of American Ballet which had been founded in 1934 by Lincoln Kirstein and George Balanchine and which was then situated on 59th Street and Madison Avenue. Beatty was the only Black pupil, pre-dating Arthur Mitchell who was to become one of the stars of Balanchine's New York City Ballet and founder of the Dance Theater of Harlem. Beatty also studied with Martha Graham, thus completing his education in the two foremost dance disciplines with the greatest choreographer/teachers working in America at that time.

Beatty continued his association with Dunham and her company for several years, as well as appearing in other Broadway shows. In 1946

▶ *Talley Beatty in a solo from Ruth Page's com-pany* Ballets Amer-icaines *which toured Europe in the 1950s.*

he danced in the revival of *Show Boat*, which also starred Pearl Primus, and in *Spring in Brazil* which, with choreography by Esther Junger, was not a success. He was featured in a minstrel-ballet, *Blackface*, choreographed by Lew Christensen for the Ballet Society which later became the New York City Ballet. During this time, Beatty has said, he was learning his craft.

A year later he was sufficiently confident to embark on a career as a concert dancer, specialising in dances that used Negro source material and jazz. He formed his own group which toured America and Europe with considerable success with a programme entitled *Tropicana*, its style and format owing quite a lot to the years Beatty had spent with Dunham and her company. It was a collection of dances based on Black themes, some going as far back as their African tribal origins, others drawing their inspiration more directly from the deep south.

During this period his choreographic style matured, the critic John Martin writing that it achieved '. . . a simplicity of manner, an integrity of approach and a sense of perspective – along with a boldness in creative adventure – that mark him as one of our substantial artists.'

In 1959 Beatty created a masterpiece, a work that is still frequently performed today in the Alvin Ailey repertoire, *The Road of the Phoebe Snow*. The Phoebe Snow of the title was a railroad train, reputedly named after a grand lady who, dressed in white satin and lace, travelled on the Lackawanna Railroad Line, looking out with disdain on the passing scene. Doubtless the work is rooted in Beatty's childhood or adolescent memories, reflecting aspects of life – and death – in the Black ghetto on the 'wrong side of the tracks'.

The following season saw the premiere of another fine work, *Come and Get the Beauty of It Hot*, to another score drawn from jazz sources, and which includes the sections 'Congo Tango Palace' and 'Toccata', which the critic John Martin described as 'extraordinarily beautiful ... full of human relations and implications but essentially an abstraction'. 'Congo Tango Palace' entered the repertoire of the Joel Hall Dancers of Chicago, a jazz-based company, with great success in 1988.

Several of Beatty's later works were less abstract, more explicitly concerned with racial injustice, discrimination and the social evils proceeding therefrom, such as violence. A typical work was *Montgomery Variations*, which dealt with the atmosphere of aggression fostered by racial discrimination. There was no particular story or narrative, just the depiction of pain, physical and psychological. Another was *Black Belt*, premiered in New York in 1969, based on the harsh realities of life in the Black ghetto, a work that pulled no punches with a powerful impact that was undiminished when it was televised by National Education Television.

Besides an extensive repertoire for the concert stage, Beatty has choreographed many sequences for stage drama and musicals, including Jean Genet's play *The Blacks*, the musical *Fly Blackbird* and a revival of *House of Flowers*, and an Afro-American transposition of Lewis Carroll's *Alice in Wonderland* entitled *But Never Jam Today*.

Beatty has been Artist in Residence at the Elma Lewis School of Fine Arts in Roxbury, Massachusetts, and his services as a teacher are in constant demand in schools and with various modern dance companies. His work as a choreographer has enriched the repertoires of many companies throughout the world, including the Alvin Ailey American Dance Theater, the Inner City Dance Company, the London Contemporary Dance Theatre, the Cullberg Dance Company in Sweden and the Batsheva Dance Company in Israel. His thematic range is as wide as Ailey's, ranging from classicism to jazz, but in the final analysis it is his works dealing either explicitly or implicitly with the Black experience, and based on Afro-Cabibbean material, which have had the most influence and the greatest force.

26

Geoffrey Holder

Born in the small British-governed island of Trinidad, just off the coast of Venezuela, Geoffrey Holder became a dancer, choreographer and painter mainly by copying his elder brother Boscoe, who also excelled in those arts. Although in that island community, it was the expected and accepted thing for young men to aim for a 'safe' career as civil servant, doctor or lawyer, and the arts were hardly a commonplace element in everyday life, Holder's parents were sufficiently enlightened to encourage their sons to pursue their artistic inclinations, however precarious or financially insecure they might appear.

Geoffrey Holder made his debut as a dancer at the age of seven, dancing the Lindy Hop with his sister in a show organised by Boscoe. It is interesting to note that, in an island where the Afro-Caribbean dance tradition was strong and which had already spawned the talents of Pearl Primus and Percival Borde, Holder's first public performance – albeit at that early age – was in a popular dance of the time rather than something more indigenous or traditional.

Later, Holder used his brother's paints to create his own pictures and although he invoked fraternal fury (it was war-time and oil paints were both expensive and difficult to obtain), his artistic talent was immediately recognised and he was offered an exhibition in the local library. As a result his talents as a dancer and a painter developed simultaneously.

When Geoffrey was eighteen Boscoe packed his bags and went to London where he formed a new Black company which toured Europe with great success. Geoffrey was left in charge of the Trinidadian company Boscoe had formed and was invited to represent Trinidad in the first pan-Caribbean Carnival, held at San Juan, Puerto Rico, in 1952. The company's performances were such a success that Holder was invited back with a smaller group of dancers to appear at the new Hilton Hotel at St Thomas in the Virgin Isles.

It was during these performances in the Virgin Isles that Holder and his company were seen by Agnes de Mille who was so enthusiastic about their dancing that she arranged for them to audition for the impresario Sol Hurok in New York. It was in this way that Holder first obtained his American visa. Hurok was unimpressed but within a short time Holder and his dancers had been engaged to appear in *House of Flowers* – that ill-fated musical in which so many of its Black cast were later to become celebrated choreographers.

Amongst the cast of *House of Flowers* was a beautiful young woman Carmen de Lavallade who had danced with the Lester Horton company in Los Angeles. Within four days of meeting her Holder had proposed and they were married. Their careers developed in parallel, de Lavallade dancing with the companies of John Butler, Alvin Ailey, Glen Tetley and Donald McKayle, with the New York City Opera and with American Ballet Theater. Holder also choreographed a concert programme for her entitled *Theater of Dance*.

But while de Lavallade worked with the foremost Black – and white – companies of the time, Holder preferred to form his own company and develop his own dance style, mainly based on the folk dances of the Carribean where he had grown up. He remains proud of the fact that he was never formally trained and he has never assimilated the dance styles of, for example, Martha Graham, John Butler, Lester Horton or Jose Limon.

When de Lavallade became pregnant and was unable to dance in the Metropolitan Opera production of *Aida*, Holder replaced her, dancing the created role of the Watusi King with notable success, so much so, in fact, that he found it advisable to engage a press agent.

It was at this time, interviewed by critics and members of the press, that it became generally known that Holder was also a serious painter. He was adamant that he did not wish to be known as 'a dancer who paints', but to be recognised as a dancer *and* a painter, pursuing two separate careers and exploiting two separate talents. He has been equally successful in both professions, showing regularly in various galleries and receiving as many accolades for his paintings and theatre designs as for his dancing and choreography. He has also had successful showings of his photography and has conducted his own radio interview programme in New York.

Apart from the dances of his native Trinidad, Holder has found inspiration in the dances of Haiti, particularly those which are based on Voodoo, or Voudoun, rituals, and he has also had a career-long interest in dances of Asian origin, especially those of India. (It is not generally known that, when slavery was abolished throughout the British Empire, hundreds of poor and destitute Indians from the Indian sub-continent were shipped to Trinidad as a substitute work force. The native dances of India, therefore, thrived alongside the Afro-Caribbean forms, making the island particularly rich in traditional folk dances.)

In his work *Dougla*, originally created for his own company and mounted for the Dance Theatre of Harlem in 1974, Holder brings together the Asian and African styles of movement which, he says, are similar in that they are 'questioning and replying through (syncopated) sounds'. In Trinidad, when Hindu and African are married, their off-spring are called 'dougla', and Holder's dance represents the ritual and celebration between two Dougla people. Holder was also responsible for the lavish setting and costumes of the work which has remained one of the most popular pieces in the repertoire of the Dance Theater of Harlem.

► *Geoffrey Holder.*

Another Holder work in the repertoire of the Harlem company is *Banda*, based on a dance of Baron Samedi, one of the most powerful of the Haitian deities, Sovereign of the Cemeteries, Lord of Eroticism, Guardian of the Past, and aristocratic King of the Clowns. Holder was also responsible for the scenery and costumes of this equally popular work.

Although Holder taught for a while at the school established in New York by Katherine Dunham, his choreography is an eclectic amalgam of those indigenous dances of Trinidad and other Caribbean islands, filtered through his own idiosyncratic way of moving, his own personal response to rhythms and music, his own imagination and creative impulse. Holder is very much his own man, something of a maverick and a rebel, highly critical of the way in which the Black race has been treated in America, yet insistent on not being labelled a Black artist. Nevertheless, for all that he is an individualist and a nonconformist, his work falls unmistakeably within the wide canon of Black dance, working within the Afro-Caribbean tradition.

27

Joel Hall

What makes Joel Hall almost unique amongst Afro-American choreographers is that his prolific output is based, in the main, on the jazz idiom – jazz music and the jazz dance vernacular as a vocabulary of movement. Moreover, whereas many choreographers both Black and white, from Talley Beatty to Jerome Robbins, have used jazz for dances of a lighthearted, rumbustious nature, Hall frequently uses the idiom for works that are deeply serious, such as *Now You See It, Now You Don't*, created in 1988 and dedicated to the plight of the homeless.

The blues, of course, have always been an element of jazz used to express the sad, even despairing side of life, but usually in the limited context of a character languishing over a lost love. Hall frequently goes much deeper, exploring the human condition in its more intense and melancholy forms, from racialism to murder.

Not that his choice of music has been limited to jazz: he has created works to the music of many varied composers, from Albinoni to Shostakovitch, but jazz remains the idiom in which he works most frequently.

Hall was born in Chicago, one of the great centres of jazz development in its early decades, an only child who was, he says, pampered and indulged by doting parents. His introduction to dance was a casual one, he just tagged along with other young people who were attending dance classes. But his obvious talent soon led to more serious study, beginning in 1966 with the modern dance teacher Francis Alice. During 1969–70 he spent several months in New York studying jazz with Nat Horne, Pepsi Bethel and Thelma Hill. Other New York teachers included Robert Christopher, a ballet teacher on the staff of the Alvin Ailey American Dance Center, and the modern teachers Michelle Murray and Trina Collins. During several months in West Germany during 1971 he also studied ballet with Heidi Hopfner.

Hall became the lead dancer in the Dance Ensemble of his *alma mater*, Northeastern Illinois University. After leaving U N I he under-

► *The charismatic Joel Hall, Artistic Director of the Joel Hall Dancers, based in Chicago, in his ballet* Maison du Créateur de Rêves.

took further modern dance study with Nana Shineflug and for a brief time danced with her group, the Chicago Moving Company.

Around this time he met Joseph Ehrenberg, a well-known Chicago actor and Director of the Chicago City Theater Company. With Ehrenberg as Managing Director and Hall as Artistic Director, they established the Joel Hall Dancers in 1974 as a division of the Chicago City Theater. Thereafter the Joel Hall Dancers embarked on a considerable touring schedule of the Eastern United States and subsequently had a number of successful seasons at New York's prestigious Joyce Theater on Eighth Avenue.

In 1985 the company began the first of several tours of Britain, and also appeared with great success on the European continent. As this is written, negotiations are in progress for the Joel Hall Dancers to become a company in residence affiliated to a new urban arts project in Liverpool.

From 1973 to 1976 Hall taught at Shineflug's Chicago Dance Center then, in association with Ehrenburg, he opened the Joel Hall Dance Studios, teaching jazz, modern dance and classical ballet to a large clientele. In 1988 the school moved to splendid new premises, shared with the Chicago Moving Company. Recently, Hall has worked to establish international scholarships for foreign students interested in studying American jazz styles.

Although by far the largest part of the Joel Hall Dancers' repertoire is devoted to Hall's choreography, it also contains major works by such internationally renowned choreographers as Ruth Page, Paul Sanasardo and Talley Beatty, whose *Month of Sundays* and *Congo Tango Palace* are particularly notable.

Apart from the many works created for his own company, Hall has choreographed Goldie Hawn's film *Wildcats*, the Chicago Opera Theater's production of Bizet's *The Pearl Fishers*, and the classically based jazz ballet *Chicago* for Chicago City Ballet.

Hall's choreography ranges widely, from the buoyant, feisty, Latin-American style of *Caliente, Por Favor*, to the Grahamesque modernism of 'Compassion', a moving duet for two males, part of a larger work, *The Sorceress*. Tall and lithe, Hall is especially impressive as a dancer in his jazz-based works such as *Nightwalker* to music by Duke Ellington, in which his height and powerful stage presence dominate the scene.

In recent years Hall has become one of the leading exponents of dance in the American mid-west, and the Joel Hall Dance Studios one of the major teaching centres in that region. As a dancer/choreographer/Artistic Director who happens to be Black Hall is naturally concerned with the artistic, social and political scene as it affects the Afro-American. But just as his company is fully integrated, with Black, White, Asian and Hispanic dancers making up its complement, so his concern is with the general human condition. One of his most affecting works, *Uhuru*, deals with the plight of Blacks in South Africa, not the United States – an example of how much of his work expresses a concern for all humanity.

28

The New Wave

There is a new generation of Black dancers and choreographers following in the wake of the major innovators like Talley Beatty, Donald McKayle and Alvin Ailey, whose work is more and more integrated with the post-modern movement.

As with their forebears, some find their inspiration in the Afro-Caribbean heritage, some in the contemporary struggle for recognition in a racially mixed, partially integrated society, and some in developing new forms of dance built upon the modern dance vocabularies that emerged half a century ago.

Bill T. Jones belongs – insofar as he belongs to any group – to this latter category. Perhaps it would be more accurate to say that he belongs to all three categories. Jones' original intention was to become an actor while he was at college on an athletics scholarship. Then he discovered dance: first Afro-Caribbean movement forms, then contact improvisation. He met Arnie Zane, a photographer, whom he encouraged to take up the contact improvisation classes. Together they became co-founders of American Dance Asylum in Binghampton, New York State, developing their careers separately, during the period 1974–6. At this time they conceived dance as spectacle: there was *Track Dance* set outdoors, with fifty extras and a plane flying overhead. Another dance was set in a parking lot, another in a huge tent, one in a cave. It was all part of that surge of environmental experiment that was part of the dance scene in the seventies.

In the late seventies Jones and Zane worked closely together, developing a number of chamber duets that juxtaposed their highly individual styles of movement: Jones more of a 'natural' dancer in the modern tradition with an athletic musculature; Zane, white-skinned, smaller, with a jerky, quirky movement style that owed little to formal training. These duets frequently made use of the spoken word, very often private confidences based on their shared lifestyle.

There was little or nothing of the Black experience in their work;

what they tended to emphasise, in the context of social progression, was overt homosexuality, a courageous 'coming-out' in dance terms. The fact that one dancer was Black and one was white was, in itself, something of a statement.

Jones and Zane produced a trilogy of duets that were among the various important influences on the post-modern dance scene of the seventies: *Monkey Run Road, Blauvelt Mountain* and *Valley Cottage*, the name of the upstate New York town where they lived together. These were highly structured, highly personal works which were very much in the current mainstream of the American dance aesthetic, drawing on the philosophy expounded by Merce Cunningham. They were works of personal exploration where each dancer was 'finding a personal way to move'.

When asked if he thought that the 'Black heritage' still influenced the American dance world, Jones replied that he thought that jazz dance reached a peak in the 1940s and that the main Afro-American influence was currently to be found amongst the young street dancers in New York. He added that, 'personally, when I move, I move as a Black man.'

After world-wide tours as a duo, Jones and Zane formed the Bill T. Jones and Arnie Zane Dancers, a group of six dancers which gradually grew to eleven. The work they created changed somewhat from highly personalised, rather narrow concepts into a wider, more exuberant, more accessible form. In 1984 they choreographed *Secret Pastures*, a riot of eclectic dance styles and with something of a plot: a Hollywood-style sub-Frankenstein story about a 'manufactured man' and an expedition to a desert isle. The work had a decor by the graffiti artist Keith Haring, an art-rock score by Peter Gordon and costumes by the designer Willi Smith. Premiered at the 2,400-seat Brooklyn Academy of Music theatre, it was an unabashed attempt to attract a new, large audience. Jones said, 'We abandoned the "high art" wagon for a while. We went for trendy instead of transcendental.' The work was a popular success although some of the critics were less enthusiastic.

In 1983 Jones choreographed a strong dance piece for six males, commissioned by the Alvin Ailey American Dance Theater which was a great success, *Fever Swamp*. In 1985 Jones and Zane collaborated on another work for the Ailey company, *Ritual Ruckus, How to Walk an Elephant*, another exuberant piece which, later, they reworked for their own company as the first part of what they called an Animal Trilogy, the other two being *Water Buffalo: An Acquired Taste*, and *Sacred Cow: Lifting a Calf Everyday Until it Becomes An Ox*. The music was a series of piano-roll studies by Conlon Nancarrow although, in the best Cun-

ningham tradition, the music seemed divorced from the choreography which appeared to derive, at least in part, from the violence and aggression of the punk movement.

On March 30, 1988, Zane died at Valley Cottage, from AIDS-related lymphoma; he was thirty-nine. His premature death, apart from being a tragic personal loss, presented Jones with both a dilemma and a challenge. In the first instant he met it by making his next work a tribute to his dead colleague and companion. How his career will continue and whether his company will remain in its present form, or at all, only time will tell.

Garth Fagan, who created the Bucket Dance Theater in Rochester, up-State New York, in 1970, has said, 'My roots are Black, but it's a cultural thing, not a racial thing. The way I really see the world is a cross-reference of cultures. Dance is a testament to people.' It is a philosophy expounded by a number of his contempories and yet Fagan has found much of his material and inspiration in Caribbean dance cultures. He was born in Jamaica, the son of an Oxford-educated government official who wanted him to follow in his academic footsteps. Fagan, however, was far more interested in the theatre and as a teenager he joined the Jamaican National Dance Theatre. At the age of twenty he left for college in the United States and subsequently studied with such leaders of modern dance as Martha Graham and Jose Limon.

Despite his adherence to modern dance techniques, the island of Jamaica and its culture is inherent in his work. 'There's a certain energy almost rampant in Caribbean dance,' he has said, 'tensile underpinnings that are kinetically inherent.' He recognises the African tradition in the Caribbean cultures and is also on record as saying, 'Imagine standing on the banks of the Congo, looking across the river. There's an awesome emotional connection. My work has its roots there.'

If the emotional roots are in Africa and the Caribbean, the artistic expression is contained in the modern dance vocabulary, although it is mixed with certain rhythmic dynamics that reflect the ethnic background. The choreographic demands that he makes on his dancers frequently include that amazing flexibility of the spine and the rotatory capability of the pelvis.

If Fagan uses the modern – and post-modern – idiom as his basic dance vocabulary he also finds much of his inspiration in the daily struggle for survival that is the common lot of most people, Black and white, in the western world. 'I'm an artist creating in the eighties,' he has said. 'The work should reflect some of the affirmations and tensions of our time.' His choreography also tends to reflect a contemporary view of men and women; of two men in his company, Steve Humphrey and A. Roger Smith, he remarks, 'They are great role models, so male, so virile, so vulnerable.' He choreographs 'broad, high jumps' for the women, saying, 'I want no "ladies" in my company. I'm tired of women who can't dance without being carried around by men. They don't live like that so why should they dance like that?'

The pop-singer Grace Jones, a fellow Jamaican, motivated Fagan's *Mask Mix Masque*, danced to songs by Jones and a taped interview, which has been a popular hit. Of Jones herself he has said, 'Despite the lip-gloss and haircut, there's a thriving primal woman. Outrageous, *au courant* and chic, there are still African roots.'

On the one hand, then, Fagan proclaims his affinity with the contemporary scene, often observed at street level; on the other his frequent references to Africa, to primal roots, to the 'kinetically inherent' traditions of Afro-Caribbean dance, betoken a continuing association with the Black dance heritage from which he draws artistic inspiration and a dynamic aesthetic.

(Overleaf) Members of the Bucket Dance Theatre Company performing Garth Fagan's work From Before.

Apart from continuing to direct his company, Fagan has taken time out to direct a version of Duke Ellington's unfinished musical *Queenie Pie* and has choreographed *Footprints Dressed in Red* for the Dance Theater of Harlem.

If Garth Fagan mixes the teachings of the great modernists such as Graham, Cunningham, Limon and Ailey with the atavistic energy of Jamaica, Jawole Willa Jo Zollar follows in the footsteps of an earlier generation, Pearl Primus and Katherine Dunham. Like them she has studied anthropology and the tribal dances of Africa which inform much of her work.

Zollar was the third of six children, her mother a blues singer, her father a real-estate man. She 'cut her teeth on scat-singing in honky-tonks resplendent with hip-swivelling, shoulder-shaking, fast-talking exotic dancers that were not "the least bit vulgar."'

Zollar received a BA in Dance from the University of Missouri at Kansas City and an MFA in Dance from Florida State University where she subsequently taught. In 1980, like so many of her associates, she moved to New York city, the centre of all dance activity in the North American continent. There she studied with Diane McIntyre and experimented with the innovative composers Craig Harris, Carl Riley and Vincent Chauncey.

In New York Zollar has given successful concert performances, and founded the dance-theatre ensemble Urban Bush Women with a repertoire based on the folklore and religious traditions of Afro-Americans and Africans. Zollar and the Urban Bush Women have appeared with considerable acclaim in Britain and Europe.

On stage Zollar has a compelling presence that belies her diminutive form. Perhaps her most forceful appearance is in her solo from *Lifedance I, The Magician (The Return of She)*, created in 1984. She comes on stage dressed as some religious eccentric, in an old lace dress, a battered hat, big boots, a huge wooden cross hung round her neck, smoking a cigar and swigging from a bottle of liquor. She utters sudden shouts and cries, cursing the devil and making wild, lurching dance steps. Gradually she dispossesses herself of her props and, her curses becoming more and more incomprehensible, she begins shaking and trembling, speaking in strange tongues; we realise she has become possessed by a demonic spirit, some Voodoo *loa* perhaps. It is a theatrical *tour de force*, supported by brilliant drumming and singing from another splendid Black artist, Edwina Lee Tyler.

Zollar's works for the Urban Bush Women range from studies of tribal dance to contemporary images of emancipated womanhood in a work such as *Girlfriends*. Zollar is just as confident in her choreographic

► *Jawole Willa Jo Zollar in her solo from* Life Dance Trilogy, *a tour de force in which, as a religious eccentric, she gradually becomes possessed by a spirit.*

portrayal of the streetwise New York working girl as she is in re-staging the tribal dances of Haiti, and in this she is somewhat unique amongst contemporary choreographers. She is arguably the most interesting and inventive of the new wave of Black choreographers, albeit working at present on a small scale. One would like to see her extend her range, choreographing perhaps for men as well as women.

These three dancer/choreographers are representative of the continuing strength of the Black dance movement. However closely it has become incorporated into the modern dance scene in general, Jones, Fagan and Zollar perpetuate the relationship with the tribal cultures of Africa and the residual influences of the Caribbean and the deep south, tributaries which constantly enrich the mainstream of American dance.

29

A Case History

From the beginning of the century, right through to the Civil Rights disorders of the sixties, a number of Black artists, dancers, musicians and singers, managed to escape from the ghettoes of the big cities and achieve a certain degree of emancipation through the theatre and the arts. The savage segregation laws still affected them in much of their daily lives but many of them managed to build a satisfying career through the resourceful exploitation of their talents. Wilbert Bradley is just one example, a case history that is representative of many others.

Bradley was born in Jackson, Mississippi, on April 28, 1926. He had a white mother and a Black father, a wholly inadmissible union at that time, and soon after the baby's birth the mother was taken from her son and 'run out of town' by the local sheriff, rejoining her family in Chicago. The baby was brought up by his aunts, who were school-teachers, and his father, who was a trumpet player with a local orchestra. As a small boy Bradley was regularly taken to the dance halls where his father was playing and would 'dance and clown' to the music.

Throughout his early years Bradley's mother kept in close touch, sending him presents and clothes and then, at the age of twelve, he made the journey north to visit his mother. It was a happy reunion and after returning to Jackson Bradley once more made the trip to Chicago, this time staying to study at the Corpus Christi School. Later, at the Du Sable High School, Bradley began studying medicine. At the same time he joined a local dance school, partly to perform with the school performing arts group called The High Jinks. At his dance school he was taught tap, which he dismissed as 'too Uncle Tom-ish', and classical ballet which he also felt was pointless because 'everybody knew Blacks didn't get into ballet'.

While continuing his medical studies at Wilson Junior College, he also worked as an usher at Chicago's Regal Theater and Savoy Ballroom where he was excited by the many Black artists he saw performing.

During the summer of 1944 he decided he wanted to travel; he took

▶ *Wilbert Bradley in an exuberant solo from* Le Ballet de Savage *to music by Les Baxter*.

a job as a waiter on the famous Chicago-Los Angeles train, the Santa Fe Chief. He was thrilled to find himself in Hollywood where, after a number of trips, he made friends with a group of people who encouraged him in his secret ambition to be a 'performer'. During one of these trips he saw Katherine Dunham's company, an experience that crystallised all his ideas about going on the stage.

With the encouragement of his dance teacher Bradley auditioned for Dunham's company when it played in Chicago. Not knowing any better, Bradley turned up at the audition in a leotard, net stockings and pointe shoes, thinking it was the appropriate costume for all dancers. Dunham asked him to show her what he could do; he managed a shaky arabesque and a wobbly pirouette which caused considerable amusement. Dunham told him to take off his costume and asked the company ballet master to set a few jazz-style steps for the young man to attempt. These he executed with a natural exuberance and rhythm and on the strength of this performance he was awarded a scholarship to the Dunham school in New York. In order to pay for his daily subsistence Bradley took a job as a short-order cook. His teachers at the Dunham school were Lavinia Williams and Talley Beatty. After a period of study at the school, Bradley was taken into Dunham's company.

The first tour that Bradley undertook with Dunham meant a year's sojourn in Mexico. During this time Bradley became, he says, 'slowly serious' about his work as a dancer. Up until then it had been fun, a sudden release into the nonconformist, fast-paced world of the theatre where, traditionally, tolerance of the individual and his preferences was far wider than in the regular working world. Up until then Bradley had been something of a maverick, a rebel, delighting in the new-found freedom to give reign to his extrovert personality. Suddenly his career, the demands of his profession, were something to be taken seriously.

From Mexico the company went to Hollywood where it performed at Ciro's Club for a season, after which the impresario Sol Hurok arranged for Dunham's first, sensationally successful, season in London. From London the company travelled to Paris where their success was even more spectacular. On the first night the cast were joined on stage by Josephine Baker (who promptly dubbed them her 'children'), Mistinguette, Jean Cocteau, Jean Marais, Jean Babilée and a host of other celebrities. During his stay in Paris Bradley, who was already proficient in Spanish, also became fluent in French. The European tour continued with visits to Italy and the Scandinavian countries before returning to New York and another season on Broadway. After Broadway came another tour organised by Hurok, this time Uruguay, Paraguay, Chile, Peru and Argentina.

Despite the company's world-wide success, Dunham was running short of money, so she flew her dancers to Jamaica for three months where they lived frugally on a small retainer and the hospitality of friends. From Jamaica Dunham took her company to the huge plantation she owned in Haiti, Chez Pauline Leclerc's, originally owned by Napoleon Bonaparte's sister. At this time Dunham restructured the company and put together a new show which was taken for a second visit to London followed by another extensive European tour. During this tour the company were also engaged to appear in the film *Mambo*, produced by Dino De Laurentis, directed by Robert Rossen and with choreography by Dunham. The tour ended in Casablanca in 1954 where Bradley decided to part company with Dunham.

Returning to Italy Bradley, together with another Dunham dancer Julie Robinson, was offered the role of lead dancer in Walter Chiari's comedy show. After a year with this organisation Bradley formed a small group of his own which gave jazz-based performances in night-clubs throughout Europe and the Middle-East, including Egypt and Iran. After this Bradley returned to the United States where he pursued a freelance career for some time before making yet another visit to Italy. This visit turned out to be a stay of some fifteen years during which he performed as a dancer, singer and actor. He also worked as a choreographer on several Italian films, included being assistant to Hermes Pan on the film *Cleopatra*. Bradley also worked extensively as an actor in Italian films and on television before finally returning to the United States in 1968.

His long stay in Italy meant that Bradley was relatively unknown in America. He decided to concentrate on acting and became a member of the Free State Theater company funded by the Goodman Institute and the National Endowment for the Arts. With this company Bradley toured all over the United States and was engaged on yet another extended European tour. Bradley stayed with this company, acting, singing, dancing and choreographing, until 1978.

For some years Bradley continued working as a freelance actor. In recent years he has worked extensively with the underprivileged, teaching various forms of dance to senior citizens, the blind and the retarded. For example, if a young person walks in a certain way through some affliction, Bradley turns that idiosyncratic movement into a dance step. He has held seminars on working with the handicapped, he works in conjunction with the Chicago Mayor's office, he is resident choreographer at the Kennedy-King College and he works with the E T A Black Theater group. Bradley's career continues to be full, varied and creative; it is a career he has built himself from humble beginnings, working hard, developing his talents, a free-ranging spirit who has escaped from a world of injustice and prejudice and the poor prospects usually attendant upon those evils. Now he is giving back to his community some of the wisdom he has learnt along the way.

30

Black Ballet

During the 1930s there were one or two ill-fated attempts to establish some form of so-called 'Negro ballet', none of which amounted to anything of consequence. The first classically trained Black dancer who achieved both status and recognition was Janet Collins who became the prima ballerina of the Metropolitan Opera House in New York from 1951 to 1954. Her performances there, and her subsequent history as a concert artist, disproved the belief of the *New York Times* critic John Martin that the 'European outlook, history and technical theory' of classical ballet was alien to Black dancers 'culturally, temperamentally and anatomically'.

Collins was born in New Orleans in 1917, but her early ballet training was in Los Angeles with Lester Horton and Carmalita Maracci. While still in Los Angeles Collins auditioned for Colonel De Basil's Ballets Russes but was not accepted because of her colour; she was told that either special parts would have to be created for her or she would have to paint her face white. Later, in New York, a special part was found for her, the role of an Ethiopian in *Aida*.

During her years with the Metropolitan Opera she also danced in Bizet's *Carmen* and the Bacchanale of Saint-Saens' *Samson and Dalilah*. During this same period she studied classical ballet with Margaret Craske and Antony Tudor, and modern dance with Hanya Holm and Doris Humphrey. She also did some teaching herself at the School of American Ballet, at Marymount Manhattan College and at the San Francisco Ballet School. Janet Collins was given the prestigious Dance Magazine Award in 1959.

The real breakthrough into ballet came when Arthur Mitchell joined the New York City Ballet in 1956 and subsequently became one of the company's most successful – and popular – soloists. Prior to joining NYCB Mitchell had already appeared with the companies of Donald McKayle and John Butler.

Mitchell was born in New York, the eldest of five children for

▶ *Janet Collins, the first classically trained Black dancer to achieve recognition, prima ballerina of the Metropolitan Opera House from 1951 to 1954.*

whom, at the age of twelve, he became the breadwinner, doing paper rounds and working as a janitor. Mitchell first began studying ballet in his late teens, and at his graduation from the High School of Performing Arts in New York (the establishment which inspired the television series *Fame*), he won the coveted Dance Award which resulted in the offer of scholarships to both Bennington College and the School of American Ballet. He chose the latter which led directly to his acceptance as a member of New York City Ballet. His debut was in Balanchine's *Western Symphony* to the music of Hershy Kay. John Martin, writing in the *New York Times*, noted the appearance of 'the talented young Negro dancer', but that was the extent of his criticism.

Mitchell's rise through the ranks of the company was rapid, however, and Balanchine created several special roles for him, such as the fiercely difficult and innovative pas de deux in *Agon* to the score by Stravinsky, and the role of Puck in his two-act version of *A Midsummer Night's Dream* to the incidental music of Mendelssohn. Despite his general acceptance as a classical dancer of great brilliance he still encountered a considerable amount of prejudice because of his colour. For example, he was not allowed to dance the role he had created in *Agon* for a commercially sponsored television transmission, because television stations in the south would refuse to carry the show and advertisers would not like that. Mitchell's pre-eminence in ballet was the exception that proved the rule: Black dancers did not appear in ballet because there still remained considerable prejudice about training for an art so associated with the white European cultural mainstream.

Mitchell remained with NYCB for fifteen years, and left the company in 1966 to appear in several Broadway shows and to act as Artistic Director of a company formed to appear at the annual Festival of Two Worlds, founded by Gian-Carlo Menotti in Spoleto, Italy.

In 1968, learning of the assassination of Martin Luther King in Memphis, Tennessee, Mitchell returned from Brazil, where he had established the National Ballet Company, determined that he should dedicate the rest of his career to the cause of Black people in the United States, in particular the Black population of Harlem where he, privileged because of his tremendous talent, had grown up.

Mitchell was convinced that, given the talent and with proper training, Blacks could excel in ballet. He said, 'We have to prove that a Black ballet school and a Black ballet company are the equal of the best of their kind, anywhere in the world.' And he set out to give a practical demonstration of his belief.

With financial help from the Ford Foundation and with Karel Shook as Associate Director, Arthur Mitchell founded the Dance Theater of Harlem as a school of allied arts and a professional dance company. Initially, the school was housed in a garage and the basement of a church belonging to the Harlem School of Arts. At the beginning there were about thirty students; by the end of that first summer there were nearly four hundred – many of whom had walked in off the street because the doors of the garage were open for light and ventilation. Modern dance was taught by one of Martha Graham's most celebrated dancers Mary Hinkson; Pearl Reynolds taught ethnic and the Dunham technique, and Mitchell and Shook took classical classes.

After relations with the Harlem School of Arts became strained, Mitchell opened his own independent school on the advice of and with help from George Balanchine and Lincoln Kirstein. With new financial support the school and the company were able to move into new premises where the school functioned with growing success under Mitchell's dynamic direction.

The first performances by the Dance Theater of Harlem were given at the Guggenheim Museum in 1971. The early repertory included several works by Mitchell, such as *Holberg Suite, Tones* and *Fête Noir*, which gave the dancers the 'feel' of neo-classical ballets and semi-ethnic works without imposing impossibly difficult technical hurdles for the embryo company. Yet within a short while the dancers were tackling ballets by George Balanchine which he had given the company, and dancing them with the panache and bravura associated with the New York City Ballet. Mitchell's vision had been substantiated.

The Dance Theater of Harlem gave its first Broadway season in 1974 at the Uris Theater, and in that same year it made a sensationally successful debut at Sadler's Wells Theatre in London, the beginning of a continuing love affair with British fans. In 1981 the company made history with its first season at the Royal Opera House in Covent Garden.

The company's British successes have been repeated all over the world, throughout Europe, the West Indies, Australia and Japan, and its repertoire has become wide-ranging, with ballets by Balanchine, Jerome Robbins, Glen Tetley, Eugene Loring, John Taras, Geoffrey Holder, Garth Fagan, John McFall, Alvin Ailey and Billy Wilson, mixed in with others from the classic and Diaghilev repertoires.

Amongst this eclectic assemblage perhaps the most interesting is Mitchell's conception of a famous Romantic work from the early nineteenth century, *Giselle*, relocated amongst the Creole and Black populace of New Orleans. Staged by Frederic Franklin, the ballet was given its world premiere at the Coliseum in London in 1984 and immediately received acclaim as a triumph of imaginative staging. Embodying the social and racial divisions of Creole society mixed with the freed slaves of the French and Spanish colonialists, the ballet seemed to have even more relevance for modern audiences than the vague, medieval Rhineland location of the usual versions. And Albert's (Albrecht's) second-act entrance in a boat, gliding across a bayou hung with Spanish moss, was as atmospheric as the moonlit glade that is the commonplace setting. With this full-length classical work Mitchell could claim to have achieved the apotheosis of Black ballet.

During its first two decades the Dance Theater of Harlem has been universally acknowledged as one of the world's finest ballet companies. But more than that it has given a sense of pride to the district of Harlem itself which is home to one of America's major cultural establishments.

▲ *Eddie Shellman as Albert (Albrecht) and Virginia Johnson as Giselle in Frederic Franklin's staging of the famous nineteenth-century classic set amongst the Creole and Black society of New Orleans.*

▶ *Arthur Mitchell as Puck, the role he created in George Balanchine's ballet* A Midsummer Night's Dream *for New York City Ballet.*

▲ *John Alleyne, soloist and choreographer, with the National Ballet of Canada in Balanchine's* Four Temperaments. *Like his colleague Kevin Pugh, Alleyne prefers to be thought of simply as a dancer rather than a Black dancer.*

Most importantly, perhaps, it has proved that there is no area of dance in which Black artists cannot excel.

Given the lead by DTH, Black dancers are beginning to appear with more and more classical ballet companies. To give just two instances, the National Ballet of Canada has two celebrated principals in Kevin Pugh and John Alleyne, while London Festival Ballet (now the English National Ballet) have Denzil Bailey, Patrick Lewis and Brenda Edwards as frequent guest artists. It must be said that almost without exception, these and many other Black dancers in other classical companies throughout the world all consider themselves to be dancers first and foremost; the colour of their skins, if not exactly irrelevant, is of secondary importance. At long last, it would seem, integration in classical dance has been achieved, just as it has long been established in various forms of modern dance.

31

Black Dance in Britain

Overleaf: Namron (centre left), whose real name was Norman Murray, was an early member of London Contemporary Dance Theatre, in Robert North's humorous and athletic Troy Game.

Originally from Jamaica, Namron was one of the first Black dancers to join a British company. His splendid physique and virile presence encouraged other young males, Black and white, to take up dancing as a career.

Because there was no indigenous Black population until after World War II, when immigration from Africa, the West Indies and other Caribbean islands began on a large scale, Black dance in Britain took a long time to get established on a firm basis. Moreover, modern dance – that is, dance movement based on the Martha Graham technique, together with the styles developed by her contemporaries and pupils – did not take root until the mid-sixties when Ballet Rambert (now Rambert Dance Company) changed from a classical to a modern company, and London Contemporary Dance Theatre was formed. And it was the modern dance companies which first began to accept Black dancers.

Before that, however, there had been one conspicuously successful attempt to produce a Black dance company with a style based on Afro-Caribbean dance, which foundered both because of lack of funds and the premature death of its creator.

Berto Pasuka was born in Kingston, Jamaica, in 1920. In his teens he dutifully obeyed his father's suggestion that he should study to become a dentist but he reacted so badly when he first saw an extraction at close quarters it was apparent that he had to seek another form of livelihood. He had already spent some time with the Maroon Negroes, descendants of runaway slaves, who had taught him some of their dances, and then, after dancing the part of a Black peasant woman at the Ward Theatre in Kingston (one is reminded of Hemsley Winfield performing Salome's Dance of the Seven Veils early in his career) he became convinced that his destiny was in the realm of dance, whatever the difficulties or cost, financial or personal.

He gathered around him a number of schoolboy friends and with them as an amateur troupe he performed native songs and dances for tourists with some success.

Pasuka read every book he could about dance which at that time was almost inevitably classical ballet. He read Tamara Karsavina's

autobiography, *Theatre Street*, and biographies and memoirs about Diaghilev, Nijinsky and the Ballets Russes which convinced him that he must make the journey to Europe to see ballet at first hand. With his small savings and a cabin trunk filled with his possessions, he landed at Liverpool on a grey, drizzly day in 1939. Almost immediately he contracted influenza and the cost of treatment consumed almost all his savings. He arrived in London weakened by his illness, with very little money and no prospects. He found work as a painters' and sculptors' model in Chelsea where his fine head and athletic physique attracted a number of artists, and he managed a day-to-day, hand-to-mouth existence throughout the years of World War II.

In his spare time and with what little money he had he went to any theatrical performance that included dancing; he also took a number of classical ballet lessons with Anna Northcote but came to the conclusion that such a formalised conception of dance could not be the basis of the choreography he wanted to create.

Pasuka's big break came when he was cast as a dancer in the film *Men of Two Worlds* (American title *Witch Doctor*) directed by Thorold Dickinson. It was a semi-documentary story set in Tanganyika in which an educated native assisted white colonialists to counter the force of witch doctors and persuade tribes to leave an infected area. With three other Black artists Pasuka improvised a scene where they danced around a camp fire; it was performed with such feverish abandon that it astonished the studio personnel and became one of the most memorable scenes in the film. More importantly, it gave Pasuka the impetus to form a nucleus of dancers who would eventually become the Ballets Nègres.

Pasuka frequented cafes, bars and clubs where other Black immigrants congregated in order to recruit for his company. Some of them had had experience as cabaret dancers, others saw the opportunity of a permanent job that also offered artistic expression. For three months, in a gloomy cellar near Piccadilly Circus, Pasuka demonstrated, bullied and coached his dozen or so aspiring dancers until he had moulded them into a cohesive company, dancing to elaborate drum rhythms supplemented by piano scores written by Leonard Salzedo, the British composer and musician who had agreed to become Pasuka's Musical Director.

Pasuka used up nearly all the money he had made from the film giving his dancers and musicians a daily travelling allowance and midday sandwiches and coffee. A further source of money came from the BBC which was interested in Pasuka's scheme of establishing a Black dance company and invited him to give radio talks to Jamaica.

Pasuka created four works for the Ballets Nègres' first eight-week

► *Berto Pasuka as the Witch Doctor and Patricia Clover as the Nurse in Pasuka's ballet* They Came.

season beginning on April 30, 1946, at the small Twentieth Century Theatre in London's Bayswater district, dancing the leading role in each one. In *De Prophet* he was the prophet of the title who cures a man of blindness and, believing in his own magical powers, dies in an attempt to fly. The second work was *They Came*, based upon the story of a witch doctor arrested by the British authorities in Jamaica; *Aggrey* was based upon the teachings of an African philosopher who believed it was only fear which separated the Black and white races (Pasuka's idea for Salzedo's score was that the black and white notes of the piano should symbolise racial harmony), and *Market Day* which, as the title indicates, reflected the colourful bustle of a Jamaican market.

The first season of the Ballets Nègres was a triumph with sold-out houses and frenzied applause each night from the audience. (Diaghilev's great ballerina, Tamara Karsavina, who was at that time living in London, refused to leave the theatre until she had been taken backstage to meet Pasuka.) This success led to another London season, this time in the West End at the Playhouse Theatre, which was equally triumphant. After that Pasuka embarked on a strenuous tour of Britain followed by an extensive tour of Europe where, if anything, his reception was even more enthusiastic. In Copenhagen, in the depths of winter, he was met at the airport by huge crowds who greeted him with flowers and music. In Amsterdam the theatre was immediately sold out with seats commanding high prices on the black market. On the first night so many people besieged the box office that the management arranged for members of the public to be accommodated in the orchestra pit.

Back in London Pasuka realised he could not recline on his laurels and he created a second programme of ballets. With Dame Sybil Thorndike as his champion he attempted to make the Ballets Nègres self-supporting as a non-profitmaking organisation, but these plans did not come to fruition. The Arts Council also refused to support him with a subsidy. (There is acute irony in the fact that, thirty years later, Stephen Dwoskin's memorial film to Pasuka, *Ballet Black*, was made under the auspices of the Arts Council.) In all, without capital and subsisting entirely on box-office receipts, the Ballets Nègres lasted for some six years, giving its last performance late in 1952. Disillusioned, Pasuka went to Paris to study painting. He returned to London in 1959, planning to resuscitate the company with a full-length work based on the life of a Haitian slave who rose to become king. In 1963 he was rehearsing a role in a production of Sean O'Casey's play *Cock-a-Doodle Dandy* when he died suddenly in what has been called 'mysterious circumstances'. He was found dead in his room with the door locked on the inside. Friends maintain that he was excited by his part in the play and had no reason to commit suicide, and there are dark hints of foul play. There seems to have been no further investigation of the matter.

With Pasuka's death there also died the prospect of establishing a permanent British Black dance company for a number of years. Like Asadata Dafora in America, Pasuka had been a decade or two before his time.

Fourteen years after Pasuka's death the Arts Council and the Greater London Arts Association were providing limited sums in support of another Black dance venture, MAAS Movers. The title derived from the Minority Arts Advisory Service under whose auspices the company was formed in March 1977, by which time of course there was a comparatively large Black population in several major British cities – indeed, there was a generation already growing to maturity for whom Britain was the homeland.

MAAS Movers was formed by some ten committed Black dancers who were aware that there was no existing Black dance company to provide a focus for young Blacks who wished for a career as professional dancers, other than cabaret and the commercial theatre. These ten dancers started to take classes regularly under the supervision of Ray Collins, an American dancer who had been Director of the junior company of the Dance Theatre of Harlem, and who had settled in Britain and was appearing in the musical *Bubbling Brown Sugar*. Collins taught classical ballet, Evrol Puckerin from Trinidad taught jazz and Afro-Caribbean styles, and Greta Mendez also from Trinidad and a graduate from the London School of Contemporary Dance taught the Martha Graham Technique. Mendez and Puckerin were appointed Associate Directors with Collins as Artistic Director.

The first performance by MAAS Movers was in the small Oval House Theatre in South London in July 1977. The programme began with a lecture demonstration conducted by Collins using the six women and four men who at that time constituted the company. It was followed by five other pieces choreographed by Collins, Puckerin and Mendez. Collins created *Women in Journey*, which attempted a sense of progression implied by the title, ranging from a pas de six for the women alone to a pas de deux for the dancer Polly Allen Smith with Collins, a somewhat conventional athletic coupling. Puckerin contributed *Lament and Confusion*, a sequence of dances for six members of the company to music by Quincy Jones for the television series *Roots*, and *Spirits*, a sort of black mass with much lighting of candles and burning of incense and a certain form of frenetic movement. Mendez performed two solos, a short piece entitled *In Limbo* and an acrobatic piece *The Chair and Me*, balancing on, around and across a chair.

The critics gave the company a cautious welcome, realising that the premise should be encouraged but also that, initially, the programmes had to be built around the limited technical abilities of some of the cast. After its short London season MAAS Movers went on a tour of the regions, particularly those cities where there were fairly large Black communities.

◀ Greta Mendez (fore-ground) and Polly Allen Smith in Women in Journey *choreographed by Ray Collins for the MAAS Movers, an all-Black company which had a brief existence in London during the 1970s.*

From the beginning the company was beset with problems. It was desperately underfunded, which meant that it was difficult to find adequate administrative staff, let alone provide the dancers with the sort of salaries they could expect in the commercial theatre, and – like several other small dance companies – it lacked a·choreographer-Director of outstanding talent.

For its second London season at Riverside Studios in Hammersmith, the company enlisted the help of the distinguished American dancer William Louther who had been a leading member of Martha Graham's company before settling in Britain and making guest appearances with the London Contemporary Dance Theatre. For MAAS Movers he created a work called *Peace be Still*, a half-hour work that took its theme from a revivalist meeting. After Collins had resigned from the position of Artistic Director, Louther was appointed as Artistic Advisor, but his next work for the company, *Praeludium and Events*, which dealt with an obscure myth, the *Epic of Gilgamesh*, was poorly received.

Inevitably, MAAS Movers disintegrated after a couple of years. Not only were there continual financial problems but the dancers themselves, who worked together as a collective, could not agree on the sort of company identity they wished to create. Some, having been trained in the Graham technique, wanted to concentrate the repertoire on modern works, avoiding being labelled as Black dancers; others considered that as their raison d'etre and wanted to create works that drew their inspiration from the Afro-Caribbean heritage. The standard of dancing remained very uneven, as did the quality of the works themselves; it proved difficult to find a Black administrator or technician for the company, and altogether, the lack of direction, the lack of identity, the lack of financial support, the lack of a company choreographer capable of creating a really outstanding repertoire all contributed to the early demise of the MAAS Movers.

Greta Mendez, one of the best dancers in the company, joined forces with another dancer who had appeared briefly with MAAS Movers, the American-born Michael Quaintance, to form the Nin Dance Company. The title came from the 'Ninth breather of emptiness', derived from a mystical novel that Quaintance was writing at the time. Somewhat less esoterically, his avowed objective for the company was 'to choreograph works that have the same power and vibrancy as the streets of Chicago', the city in which he grew up. The company performed on the fringe of London for a season or two with some success, before joining MAAS Movers in oblivion. It was not until the mid-eighties that two new Black companies, each with very distinct identities, were formed and proved that they could exist as viable propositions.

Irie! (the title is taken from a word of greeting, common throughout the Caribbean) evolved as part of a year-long programme entitled Caribbean Focus devised to illustrate the rich Caribbean cultural heritage that existed within local communities in south London. When the year, 1984, was over Irie!, whose performances had proved tremendously popular, continued in existence, expanding and developing as a dance company whose work is based on Caribbean and jazz dance forms.

The Artistic Director and company choreographer is Beverley Glean who was born in Grenada and came to live in London at the age of five. Her interest in dancing was fostered at school by a physical training instructor who was also a passionate devotee of modern dance. As a result of her influence, Glean subsequently attended the three-year dance course at the Laban Centre for Movement and Dance at Goldsmith College where, she says, she learnt a 'mish-mash of styles'. Later she attended a six-week summer school held at the Jamaica School of Dance in Kingston, Jamaica.

Following work in various outreach projects in dance and drama under the auspices of the Inner London Education Authority, Glean was appointed Dance Development Officer at the Albany Empire Theatre in south London, and her work with young dance students there provided the basis for Irie! when it was formed in 1984.

Since then the company has developed regular programmes with funding provided for particular projects by the Arts Council and the Greater London Arts Association as well as the local council, regional councils and private sponsorship.

With a cast of eight dancers, the company embarked on its most ambitious project late in 1988, a full-length production based on the Orpheus myth, transposed to a Caribbean setting and with a reggae score, entitled *Orfeo ina Night Town*. It was presented at The Place in London, home of London Contemporary Dance Theatre, as well as various venues throughout the city. The work received very favourable reviews from the critics and played to packed houses. A world-wide tour, including Europe, the USA, Japan, Australia and the Caribbean was undertaken in 1989 with great success.

While Irie! pursues a policy of integration, the fact that it draws almost exclusively upon Caribbean themes for its repertoire has meant, in practice, that its dancers are Black, and its future may be seen as a Black dance company promoting the Afro-Caribbean cultural heritage from its London base.

By contrast, Adzido Pan-African Dance Ensemble, as its name implies, is based upon many forms of tribal dance emanating from the African continent. In the Ewe language of Ghana, *adzido* means 'oak tree, around whose girth no single man can reach' – the deliberate image of a company whose members are drawn from a dozen different countries throughout the African continent.

Adzido was formed by George Dzikunu in 1984, the same year as Irie!, and has developed with equal rapidity and success. Dzikunu was born in Ghana where his father, grandfather and other family members were master drummers of the Anlo tribe in the Volta region of the country, so that from an early age dancing and drumming were an intrinsic part of his life. He finished his formal education in Accra and then, in his early teens, he joined the African Theatre Troupe, affiliated to the Arts Council of Ghana. In 1967 Dzikunu took up full-time employment with the Ghana National Dance Ensemble where he studied choreography under Professor Opoku. During this period Dzikunu formed the Sankofa Dance Company which he brought to Britain in 1974. In many ways the performances of Sankofa were a great success although there were occasions when they were poorly attended through lack of promotion and publicity – a lesson well learnt when Dzikunu came to form Adzido some years later.

Dzikunu decided to settle in London with his wife and family and subsequently undertook extensive tours around the country, working as a freelance dancer and choreographer. He worked with the musical group Steel and Skin and with the Ekome Dance Company in Bristol during which time he developed choreographic and musical techniques which were communicable to very young school children. In his constant travelling around the British Isles Dzikunu provided tuition for thousands of young pupils.

When Adzido was established in 1984 the funding bodies financed a research trip to several African countries where Dzikunu identified and learnt many of the dances that were to be included in Adzido's repertoire.

By 1988 Adzido was sufficiently established to embark upon a short season at Sadler's Wells Theatre where the company played to packed and enthusiastic houses. The production was a full-length work, *Coming Home*, the story of the son of an African chief who, after some years in the west, returns to his tribe for his brother's initiation ceremony. To everyone's dismay the young man has forgotten his tribal dances – the discos have taken their toll. His father sends him on a journey around Africa so that he may re-learn the significance of dance in African society. Within the framework of this Odyssey the company of twenty-eight dancers and musicians are able to perform various dances from Benin, Nigeria, Uganda and South Africa.

Dzikunu is well aware that, like any dance company, Adzido must constantly add to its repertoire and to this end he makes regular visits to various African countries where, aided by a video camera, he discovers new dances and experts to teach them to his company. He is also acutely conscious of the need to maintain and improve standards of dancing and production. Adzido has already built an enthusiastic following throughout Britain – with as many white as Black people in the audiences – and the company is unique in displaying the cultural roots of the Afro-Caribbean tradition with which the West has long been familiar.

In direct contrast to Adzido, which shows the many tribal dances of Africa in their purest form, Union Dance, as its name suggests, provides a very varied mix of Afro-Caribbean, jazz and modern techniques, following the personal philsophy of multi-racial integration expounded by the company's founder, Corinne Bougaard.

Bougaard was born in South Africa, a 'Cape-coloured' of very mixed ancestry: Indonesian, Malaysian, Dutch and French. Her father, who was a teacher, came to Britain to avoid the vile and odious apartheid laws of the South African government. Her interest in the theatre was stimulated by her mother (the first play that Bougaard saw was, perhaps significantly, *Othello*), and she began to attend dance classes at the age of ten at a school in Leicester. Later, when the family moved to London, Bougaard spent three years at the London School of Contemporary Dance, after which she joined the London Contemporary Dance Theatre Lecture-Demonstration Group. During a period of further study she worked with the Alvin Ailey Studio in New York as well as with the Dance Theater of Harlem.

Back in London, and proficient both in classical ballet and the Graham technique, Bougaard joined Ballet Rambert (now Rambert Dance Company). After several seasons with this oldest of British dance companies she joined the Extemporary Dance Theatre, formed in 1975 as something of a satellite of the London Contemporary Dance Theatre and a smaller company committed to new forms of dance in the postmodern idiom.

With this extensive background in several forms of dance Bougaard founded Union Dance in 1983 'with the aim of producing dance theatre freed from the boundaries and limitations of one culture'. This formula has so far proved singularly successful and the company of seven racially mixed dancers has been well received throughout extensive tours of Britain and Europe. The danger of course lies in the possibility of an uneven repertoire, or of failing to establish a company identity while promoting such a mixture of styles. Future plans include working with choreographers of international stature, of incorporating contact impro-

▲ *The Union Dance
Company (founder and
Artistic Director Corinne
Bougaard, second from
left) in the work* Delirium
*by Jon Smart, performed
with the 'dub' poet Benjamin Zephaniah, centre.*

visation within the more rigid dance forms and of extending the company's outreach programmes to urban areas not served by other dance companies and thereby building new audiences. If these policies come to fruition then Bougaard and her company will have made a significant achievement in terms of artistic and racial integration within the British dance scene.

Although the Phoenix Dance Company based in Leeds does not label itself a Black dance company, nor do its dancers think of themselves in terms of the colour of their skins, the fact remains that this (currently) all-male group are perceived in those terms purely because the present Artistic Director and the five dancers happen to be Black or racially mixed.

Phoenix Dance Company was formed in 1981 by Leo Hamilton, Donald Edwards and Villmore James. A year later they were joined by Merville Jones and Edward Lynch, a partnership which lasted until 1987 when Hamilton and Jones left the company to pursue separate careers and Neville Campbell was appointed as Artistic Director. Douglas Thorpe, Gary Simpson and Junior Edwards were engaged as dancers.

In 1987 Phoenix moved into a new permanent home in the Yorkshire

▶ *Gary Simpson in the
work* Leave Him Be, *choreographed by his
fellow dancer with the
Phoenix Dance Company,
Villemore James.*

▼ *Kenneth Tharp (left) and Paul Liburd in the London Contemporary Dance Theatre production* Shift *by Jonathan Lunn.*

Dance Centre, an organisation providing dance and dance-related activities for the people of Yorkshire. The city of Leeds had pursued an enlightened policy of supporting the arts and the Harehills Middle School, in particular, incorporated dance in its curriculum which resulted in a sudden surge of accomplished young male dancers who subsequently needed an outlet for their abilities. Phoenix Dance Company was a direct result of this policy; the fact that Harehills was

located in the middle of Afro-Asian communities resulted in many young dance graduates being of Black or Asian origin. Whereas Union Dance has a deliberate policy of racial integration, Phoenix Dance Company is a small modern dance company whose members just happen to be Black. Between them they represent the growing integration of dancers of whatever race or colour on the British dance scene.

Phoenix Dance Company envisages recruiting female dancers in the future; for the present it has had considerable success with a repertoire that exploits their male capabilities and personalities. Three of the five dancers – Donald Edwards, Edward Lynch and Villemore Jones – as well as the Artistic Director, Neville Campbell, have choreographed works for the company, ranging from *Leave Him Be* by Jones, based on the rigours and pressures of touring, of one-night stands in small, cold halls, to *X3* by Campbell, which explores the relationship between the three elements, earth, fire and water, and time. Phoenix has also worked with several outside choreographers, such as Darshan Singh Bhuller, David Glass and Jane Dudley, and others will be commissioned in the future.

From its early days as an underpaid, overworked little group, living a hard, hand-to-mouth existence, Phoenix is now well supported by the Yorkshire Arts Association, Leeds City Council and Regional Arts Associations. Merely by being Black dancers and being where they are, the company represents a symbol of hope for the future of dance in Britain.

32

Conclusion

For Black dance and Black dancers the road to freedom has been long and hard, spanning some four hundred years. Yet, from the anonymous slaves who danced for their white masters to the Alvin Ailey American Dance Theater, from Juba to Bill T. Jones, from Berto Pasuka to the Phoenix Dance Company, it has been a journey in which pride has frequently overcome prejudice.

Of course, problems still remain for the Black dancer and choreographer but nowadays they are more likely to be aesthetic than political, social or racial. At convocations of Black culture such as, for example, the American Dance Festival of 1988 held at Durham, North Carolina, where the theme was The Black Tradition in American Modern Dance, the question most likely to be asked is 'What shall the Black dancer dance about?' just as it was when Hemsley Winfield performed at the Harlem YWCA back in 1933.

While some Black dancers and choreographers find inspiration in their Afro-Caribbean heritage, from Nigeria to Haiti, Benin to Trinidad, others prefer to disregard the Black label, dancing with classical ballet companies and modern groups, discovering and developing new forms of movement from breakdance to contact improvisation: the barriers are down and the world of dance is theirs to explore and exploit.

And yet ... the journey is not quite over. There is a bitter irony in the fact that the continent from which the west first received Black dance contains a political system which separates whites from Blacks both on and off stage. What, indeed, should the Black dancer dance about?

List of Works Cited

Page 9   Geoffrey Gorer, *Africa Dances*, Penguin Books, London, 1945.

Page 16   F. W. Wurdemann, *Notes on Cuba*, James Munroe and Company, Boston, 1844.

Page 20   Fernando Ortiz, *Los Bailes y el teatro de los Negros en el Folklore de Cuba*, trans. Dorothy Latasa Kiefer, **Cardenas y Cia**, Havana, 1951.

Page 23   Alfred Metraux, *Voodoo in Haiti*, Andre Deutsch, London, 1959.

Page 23   Melville J. Herskovits and Frances S. Herskovits, *Trinidad Village*, Alfred A. Knopf, New York, 1947.

Page 24   Katherine Dunham, 'Ethnic Dancing', *Dance Magazine*, September, 1946.

Page 28   Lynne Fauley Emery, *Black Dance in the United States from 1619 to 1970*, National Press Books, California, 1972.

Page 31   Ex-slave Toby Jones, recorded in *Slave Narratives*, Federal Writers' Project, Washington DC, 1936/8.

Page 34   Marshall and Jean Stearns, *Jazz Dance*, Schirmer Books, New York, 1964.

Page 44   Charles Dickens, *American Notes*, First published 1842.

Page 49   Marshall and Jean Stearns, *Jazz Dance*, Schirmer Books, New York, 1964.

Page 95   Marshall and Jean Stearns, *Jazz Dance*, Schirmer Books, New York, 1964.

Page 122 Joseph H. Mazo, *Prime Movers*, Adam and Charles Black, London, 1977.

List of Illustrations

Picture research – Vanessa Whinney

Index

Index compiled by Peva Keane

Acknowledgements

In writing this book I am indebted to a number of people whose research, reminiscences and remarks provided invaluable information.

I should like to thank Joe Nash, dancer, choreographer, teacher and archivist for his help in research and the wisdom he expounded in discussing the broad subject of Black dance.

I am indebted to Sule Greg Wilson, archivist at the Schomburg Center for Research in Black Culture, Harlem, New York City, for his invaluable help in finding research material and photographs.

I am particularly grateful to Joel Hall and Joseph Ehrenburg, of the Joel Hall Dancers and the Chicago City Theater Company, not only for their introductions to a number of distinguished dancers and choreographers, for their suggestions and information, but also for their generous hospitality while visiting Chicago.

There are numerous dancers, choreographers and artistic and company directors whom I must thank for so readily submitting to interviews and who talked freely about their lives and professions. They include John Alleyne, Talley Beatty, Corinne Bougaard, Wilbert Bradley, George Dzikunu, Beverley Glean, Geoffrey Holder, Bill T. Jones, Greta Mendez, Arthur Mitchell, Kevin Pugh, Julian Swain and Jawole Willa Jo Zollar.

Once again I am grateful to William Poole, librarian at the Royal Academy of Dancing, for the research reading so helpfully provided, and to Sue Merrett of the *Dancing Times* who produced information and research material so promptly.

Both Leonard Salzedo and Stephen Dwoskin were immensely helpful in clarifying certain aspects about Berto Pasuka and his Ballets Nègres.